W9-AVI-111

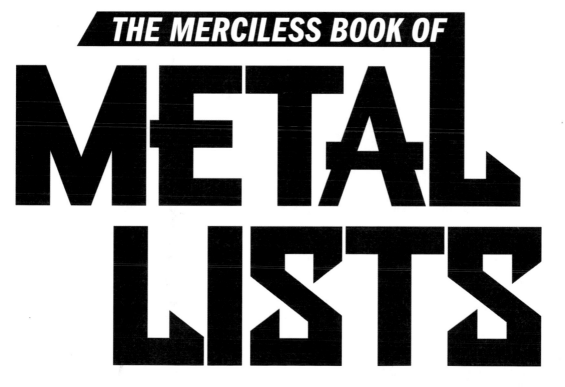

THE MERCILESS BOOK OF

METAL LISTS

HOWIE ABRAMS

SACHA JENKINS

THE MERCILESS BOOK OF
METAL LISTS

PHOTOGRAPHY BY *Frank White*

ABRAMS IMAGE, NEW YORK

Editor: David Cashion
Designer: Donna McLeer / Tunnel Vizion Media
Production Manager: Erin Vandeveer

Library of Congress Cataloging-in-Publication Data:

Abrams, Howie.
  The merciless book of metal lists / Howie Abrams & Sacha Jenkins ; photography by
Frank White (unless noted otherwise).
      pages cm
   ISBN 978-1-4197-0738-4
1. Heavy metal (Music)—Miscellanea. I. Jenkins, Sacha. II. Title.
   ML3534.A236 2013
   781.66—dc23
                                    2012042802

Text copyright © 2013 Howard Abrams and Sacha Jenkins
Photographs copyright © 2013 Frank White (unless otherwise noted)

Page 64 and 65 Illustration by MoreFrames Animation. Courtesy of ILL BILL
(taken from the music video "Paul Baloff")
Pages 67 (Ronnie James Dio) and 183 (MC Serch) by Ed Esposito.
Pages 98 and 136 courtesy of Katon W. DePena/Black Devil Records.
Page 102 (Brian Slagel) by Stephanie Cabral.
Pages 140 and 141 courtesy of Betsy Weiss.
Page 179 courtesy of Bella Kozyreva.
Pages 182 and 183 courtesy of Richard Christy.

The copyright in the original album cover designs is retained by the original record
companies, artists, photographers, and designers.

Published in 2013 by Abrams Image, an imprint of ABRAMS. All rights reserved. No portion
of this book may be reproduced, stored in a retrieval system, or transmitted in any form
or by any means, mechanical, electronic, photocopying, recording, or otherwise, without
written permission from the publisher.

Printed and bound in the United States
10 9 8 7 6 5 4 3 2 1

Abrams Image books are available at special discounts when purchased in quantity for
premiums and promotions as well as fundraising or educational use. Special editions can
also be created to specification. For details, contact specialsales@abramsbooks.com or
the address below.

THE ART OF BOOKS SINCE 1949
115 West 18th Street
New York, NY 10011
www.abramsbooks.com

CONTENTS

A MERCILESS FOREWORD BY SLAYER'S KERRY KING

If anyone had asked us when we set out on this adventure who the perfect person to serve up a foreword for *The Merciless Book of Metal Lists* would be, the answer would immediately have been "someone from Slayer," and when zeroing in on "the one," it most certainly would be guitarist Kerry King. While he arguably has half a handful of peers when it comes to authentic Metal flag bearers, he openly and boldly represents all that is pure and great about Heavy Metal music and culture.

While Sabbath invented it and Metallica flipped it into its modern form, Kerry King and Slayer burned the whole shit down and rebuilt it, incorporating the best elements of its predecessors, into the last great incarnation of Metal we all know and would die for. In the early to mid-1990s, when some believed the way to "resurrect" Heavy Metal was to add elements of other genres and create new hybrid formulas for the sound—some of which were actually pretty good, but absolutely NOT classifiable as Metal—Kerry and Co. remained steeped in the essence and followed time-honored manners to keep the anger, aggression, razor-like precision, and darkness intact while simultaneously advancing the ball. Kerry also manages to continue writing riffs that make you want to injure anyone within striking distance, which is nothing short of an art form in itself. And for that, we are eternally grateful.

While Kerry was still locked into his responsibilities to the 2012 Mayhem Festival, along with Motörhead, Slipknot, Anthrax, and others, he thankfully agreed to participate in this book via an interview. We wanted to find out more about his discovery of, and evolution through, Metal—as both a fan and musician—to illustrate how someone of Kerry King's stature and standing came to be, well, Kerry King. He's a perfect choice to set the tone for what this book is about and who it's for: REAL Metalheads! Those who are first on their block to illegally download the new [insert favorite Metal band's name here] album the second it is available for consumption from any number of sketchy online destinations, yet still purchase the album so they can properly scour through the liner notes. The fans who might scream "fucking sell-out" if an album contains even one song with a tempo one BPM slower than anything on the band's previous release. The kids who line up at the venue at ten A.M., even though doors aren't open until eight P.M. The ones who buy a tour shirt and wear it every day for the next week. That's who this book is for and that's why we asked Kerry the questions we did. Read on, maniacs!

SO, YOU GREW UP IN SOUTHERN CALIFORNIA. WHAT WERE YOU INTO AS A KID? MUSIC, SPORTS, BOTH?

KERRY: I was a music fan and also into football and baseball, but mostly football. I never really played, though. I'm not the biggest guy, so being a football fan is one thing, but playing is another. The smaller guys got crushed. Now I'm obsessed with football . . . I can tell you more about YOUR team than you'll ever know . . . and I happen to play guitar in Slayer.

AND YOU BEGAN PLAYING GUITAR WHEN?

KERRY: My dad got me a guitar when I was thirteen so I would stay out of trouble, although I'm not sure that worked. I took lessons, and while I wouldn't say I was a natural, I picked it up really quick.

WHAT WERE THE FIRST SONGS YOU LEARNED TO PLAY?

KERRY: The easy stuff. I had no technique, so I wanted to learn what I heard on the radio—Van Halen, Ted Nugent, Styx . . . stuff like that.

DID YOU HAVE ASPIRATIONS OF BEING IN A BAND EARLY ON?

KERRY: It's funny because, little did I know, my guitar teacher was actually grooming me to join his band. I was around fifteen or sixteen, and he wanted me to replace their guitar player. I eventually did, and we played some shows. I needed a fake ID just to play them. It was probably 75 percent covers, which you had to do to get gigs, and 25 percent original material. I was supernervous, by the way. I was either going to surprise or horrify.

AND WHAT WAS YOUR INTRODUCTION TO METAL?

KERRY: Again, it was what I heard on the radio, and the Heavy Metal on the radio at that time was Judas Priest. "Breaking the Law," "Living After Midnight" . . . I loved the *British Steel* album and the whole two-guitar thing. Then I went backward and copped their previous albums and became a huge Priest fan.

WHEN DID YOU SEE JUDAS PRIEST LIVE FOR THE FIRST TIME?

KERRY: I saw them after *British Steel*, on the Point of Entry tour. By then, they'd begun to get bluesier and started to have a little less of what I loved about them. Plus, they had a band called Iron Maiden opening on that tour that kicked the living hell out of them.

SO IT'S SAFE TO ASSUME THAT BY SEEING MAIDEN, AMONG OTHER THINGS, YOU REALIZED THAT THERE WERE TONS OF OTHER BANDS YOU NEEDED TO KNOW ABOUT.

KERRY: By then I was regularly reading [biweekly UK Heavy Metal/hard rock magazine] *Kerrang!* and was able to learn about a lot of bands. That's how I kept up-to-date on bands like Sabbath and Motörhead and found out about bands like Venom. All silliness aside, when I was a kid looking at pictures of Venom, Cronos was HUGE, and I thought he actually talked to Satan, like every five minutes! Any information was great information. *Metal Hammer* later on too.

WERE YOU EVER A TAPE TRADER OR DO A FANZINE?

KERRY: Never wrote a fanzine, but I traded demo tapes. That's how I got [Metallica's] *No Life 'til Leather* demo early on. Plus, at that point, I'd already found the other guys who came to make up Slayer through a local paper called the *Recycler*. They were my outlet to talk about everything we liked and didn't like about a lot of bands.

WHY DO YOU THINK, UNLIKE WITH ANY OTHER MUSIC COMMUNITY—IF YOU CAN TRULY CALL THEM THAT—METAL FANS ARE SO PASSIONATE AND CRAZY AND WANT TO KNOW ABSOLUTELY EVERYTHING ABOUT THEIR FAVORITE BANDS?

KERRY: There's something to be said about the family aspect of it. We did an in-store yesterday, and there were parents, kids . . . you didn't know who brought who. Turns out that both love the band. There's seniority involved—parents and older brothers and sisters hand it down to their kids and siblings. With hip-hop, for instance, the excitement around an artist is temporary. Even with punk. On the other hand, we have maintained a level of excellence for thirty years, and the fans appreciate and respect that.

SO HOW HAVE YOU APPLIED THAT LEVEL OF DEDICATION BACK TO SLAYER FANS?

KERRY: For one, we've never done anything just to be popular. If more bands applied that philosophy, there'd be a whole lot more happy Metal fans. We always try to leave our mark. When you write and record and release an album, you can't get those songs back. It always has to be Slayer. We're the AC/DC of Thrash. You know that what you get is going to be great and it will sound like us. Also, I don't know how it became a rule at an in-store that people can only get one thing signed . . . usually your newest album. We don't believe in that. If a kid brings fifteen things, I'm signing all fifteen. Sometimes I have to take pictures of what they bring because I've never seen it before. If the guy at the store gives me a fifteen-minute warning that the store is going to close, I let them know that if they're cool with staying open, I'll stay. I feel obligated. These people gave me a career. It would suck to have to blow off the last few people in line. In the early days, we'd only cut it short if we had a flight to catch or something like that. Most fans understand.

DO PEOPLE COME UP TO YOU TO TELL YOU WHEN SOMEONE'S TALKING SHIT ABOUT YOU ON A MESSAGE BOARD? SOME FANS TEND TO DO THAT.

KERRY: Sometimes.

WHAT DO YOU DO?

KERRY: I don't pay any attention to it. I've become immune to it. There are a lot of stupid people out there, and we know everyone feels ten feet tall behind a computer keyboard.

DO YOU THINK METALHEADS WILL APPRECIATE A REALLY OPINIONATED BOOK CREATED BY FANS, FOR FANS SUCH AS THIS ONE??

KERRY: Totally. It will appeal to them because it's what they love. They'll get to laugh at the industry and at themselves. Plus, hard-core Metal fans want everything. Even if they download an album for free, they still buy the CD, the vinyl, the picture disc . . . everything. It's a brotherhood. There's a camaraderie among Metal fans that's unlike anything else. Like I said earlier, any information is good information, and Metal kids want it.

INTRODUCTION

No music community anywhere in the world is more passionate, opinionated, and possessive than that of Heavy Metal. Its supporters regularly gut check their favorite bands and ask questions like "Is the new album HEAVIER than the last one?" "Are the solos more TECHNICAL?" "He's not SINGING more than he's SCREAMING, is he?" "Why the fuck are they touring with THEM?" The wrong answer to any of these questions draws cries of "SELLOUT" and can lead to the banishment of one's favorite band to Metal Siberia. Heavy Metal fans love to study album credits and dissect each tidbit of information available to them to keep their relationship with a band and their music as intimate as possible. God forbid if the most trendoid kid in your school catches on to your favorite band—said band becomes a silenced, rotting aural corpse.

Thankfully, we have managed to progress through our decades of Metal fandom with fairly open minds. When Metallica released their stellar sophomore effort, *Ride the Lightning*, many of our peers were up in arms over the fact that there weren't as many fast songs on the album as there were on Met's debut, *Kill 'Em All*; there was a "ballad" on the album (albeit one focused on the cheery topic of losing one's will to live), and believe it or not, some hated it simply because Metallica made a second album at all, let alone one on which they stretched their musical exploration. While we "get it," sometimes we just don't get it! In an effort to avoid being lumped in with the WRONG Metal crowd, a ridiculous array of subgenres have been hastily concocted. The Headbangers, once united under the banner of sex, drugs, and FUCKING METAL, have become divided among cliques defined by clothing, song tempos, and an artist's perceived commercial intentions (or lack thereof). What has four thumbs and is guilty of partaking in all of this? THESE GUYS!!!

With all of that, there are many UNIVERSALLY ACCEPTED TRUTHS when it comes to Metal. Similar to the way we recklessly opined via our past journalistic forays—Howie's zine, *Occasional Irregularity* (one of the greatest Metal and hard-core zines of all time), and Sacha's *Ego Trip* (one of the greatest music and culture magazines of all time)—we now set before you OUR truths. The things we believe in our hearts to be factual in regard to all aspects of OUR beloved Metal. Agree, disagree; send us death threats. We couldn't care less, because we are certain that any REAL Metalhead will agree with us. Of course, you're entitled to your opinion, but if your opinion happens to differ from ours, YOU'RE WRONG! None of these lists were assembled with the intention of hurting anyone's feelings, but we anticipate some tears being shed should your favorite band become a target. Get over it, don't take life so seriously, and KILL POSERS!

—Howie Abrams & Sacha Jenkins

heavy metal
noun

Energetic and highly amplified electronic
rock music having a hard beat

—*Merriam-Webster's Collegiate Dictionary*

Yeah, that's what THEY think. As far as we're concerned—and we believe we speak for any hard-core fan—Heavy Metal officially began with the mighty Black Sabbath. When they unleashed their self-titled debut in 1970, EVERYTHING changed! Guitar tones, lyrical content, album cover art—EVERYTHING! And let's not forget the tritone, aka satanic, chords, aka diabolus in musica. Oooooh, scary! Sabbath is the undisputed heavyweight champion of all time and stands to this day as the most influential Heavy Metal band ever. Sure, arguments can be made for the influence of bands like Led Zeppelin and Deep Purple too, but really, if you consider yourself a true Metal soldier, Black Sabbath is the be-all and end-all. Shit—so many of the kids who we (those of a certain age group) went to junior high and high school with LOVED Led Zep and Deep Purple but HATED Heavy Metal. So, as a well-deserved FUCK YOU to the haters, only direct and indirect disciples of Ozzy, Tony, Geezer, and Bill will be featured within these pages. What is Metal and what isn't is one of those grand arguments Metalheads love to engage in, and of course, there are a handful of positions you can take. This is ours, so if you don't know, now you know.

KREATORS

Pretty much since Heavy Metal's inception, there have been a number of things closely associated with it, from the clothing to the instruments to physical gestures; all are crucial elements, as they pertain to the music and the culture alike. Without them, who knows where we'd be right now. Probably listening to the Grateful Dead and wearing swirly tie-dye shit, stinking of patchouli—but that's not the point. The point is, anyone responsible for the creation of any of these deserves a pat on the back and a firm handshake of gratitude. So let's give it up.

1  **DEVIL HORNS** – Ronnie James Dio. While he did not invent the bold, extended-pointer-and-pinkie-finger gesture, he certainly brought it to the forefront and popularized it among the Heavy Metal faithful everywhere. Special shout-out to Grandma Padavona for making it happen.

2  **ELECTRIC GUITAR** – Many people credit Les Paul, but in actuality it was George Beauchamp, in conjunction with Adolph Rickenbacker. They constructed what would be the first viable electric guitar.

3  **DRUMS** – Drums were first discovered around eight thousand years ago in what is now Iraq. They were used to signal war or simply for fun.

4  **SATAN** – Satan's first appearance is in the Hebrew scriptures written before 300 BCE. The term "Satan" in those scriptures refers to one who "opposes," and when the scriptures were eventually translated into Greek and widely used by the Christian church, the term came to mean "diabolic," from which we derive "the devil." Eventually, Satan would represent anyone or anything adversarial toward God. Yeah boyeeeee.

5  **T-SHIRTS** – The T-shirt came from the separation of the nineteenth-century "union suit," worn by miners and such, into a top and bottom part. The top, now known as the T-shirt, was popularized by the Navy during the Spanish-American War, as it was more comfortable for the sailors to wear in tropical climates, and prevented them from soiling their uniform jackets.

6  **FIRE** – The first fire was most likely caused by lightning, but once it was able to be maintained and controlled, as well as re-created, humans learned of its benefits and used fire for cooking and for warmth, etc.

7  **LEATHER** – Man has been using animal hide as clothing for tens of thousands of years, if not longer.

8  **DENIM** – Originally a French serge fabric, it was dyed with indigo to make it blue and worn by miners as durable work clothing.

9  **BOOTS** – Prehistoric, origins unknown

10  **SNEAKERS** – Charles Goodyear created the first rubber galoshes in the 1840s, which eventually turned into rubber-soled tennis shoes in the early 1890s.

11  **MOTORCYCLE JACKETS** – During World War I, leather jackets were made for aviators and tank crews. When the war was over, the abundant leather jackets were converted to suit motorcyclists, to keep them safe from road rash.

IN THE NAME OF THE FATHER,
THE SON, AND THE AUTHORS

THE AUTHORS' TOP 20 METAL BANDS OF ALL TIME

As we will be talking SO much shit within these pages, it's only fair to let you know which bands we believe to be the crème de la crème, so that we may begin on the same page, so to speak.

1. BLACK SABBATH
2. IRON MAIDEN
3. METALLICA
4. SLAYER
5. MOTÖRHEAD
   (even though Lemmy believes they are simply a loud rock 'n' roll band)
6. JUDAS PRIEST
7. EXODUS
8. MANOWAR
9. VENOM
10. ANTHRAX
11. MERCYFUL FATE
12. SEPULTURA
13. CELTIC FROST
14. VOIVOD
15. NUCLEAR ASSAULT
16. TESTAMENT
17. OBITUARY
18. FEAR FACTORY
19. MÖTLEY CRÜE (YES—Mötley Crüe)
20. MEGADETH
    (even though we loathe Dave Mustaine)

Now, before you cry, "How did THEY not make the top 20?!" here are a few examples illustrating our thought process:

1. **KISS** – They've maintained all along that they strove to be a combo platter of the New York Dolls and Alice Cooper. Not Metal.

2. **AC/DC** – They may drink like Metallers, but musically, they are not. A loud, old-fashioned rock band, for sure.

3. **Guns N' Roses** – There's not a lot separating GN'R from early Aerosmith, as far as we're concerned. Drug-fueled, bluesy hard rock. Definitely not Metal.

4. **Led Zeppelin** – Led Zep is a primary example of what Metal is NOT. Heavy Metal's power comes from its stripped-down nature, never trying to be too clever, and certainly not by being based in the swampy blues.

5. **Deep Purple** – See the explanation for number 4. Big-time influence on the genre, but not an HM band.

"I don't give a shit what you say—KISS is Metal!"

MR. KAVES
BROOKLYN, NY | GRAFFITI LEGEND

20 BANDS OFTEN CONSIDERED "METAL" BUT SIMPLY <u>ARE NOT!</u>

The mere suggestion of these bands falling under the category of "Heavy Metal" is enough to make any self-respecting Headbanger want to vomit. Once the media at large grabs on to something, as they did with Metal in the '80s and early '90s, unbeknownst to most, they become experts (and in the case of Metal, every long-haired male with a guitar was considered to be one of our troopers). Thankfully, real recognizes real, and we present to you some of the bands that didn't exactly try too hard to shed the Metal label when it was the cool thing to be, yet were pretty quick to shit on it when it no longer suited them. To be fair, some were simply lumped into the genre by dopey journalists, as well as some by fans at a loss for a proper description. But you know what? None of these are real Heavy Metal bands, as far as we're concerned.

1. GUNS N' ROSES
2. KISS
3. LED ZEPPELIN (provided influence, but JNM—Just Not Metal)
4. DEEP PURPLE (see Led Zep)
5. POISON
6. DEF LEPPARD (WERE actually a Metal band early on)
7. WHITESNAKE (may have been Metal early on too)
8. ALICE IN CHAINS
9. DOKKEN
10. GREAT WHITE
11. WARRANT
12. RATT
13. VAN HALEN
14. SCORPIONS
15. AC/DC
16. NIGHT RANGER
17. EUROPE
18. CINDERELLA
19. SOUNDGARDEN
20. MARILYN MANSON

THE 10 METAL ALBUMS PLAYED MOST OFTEN DURING THE WRITING OF THIS BOOK

1. METALLICA – Ride the Lightning
2. SLAYER – Hell Awaits
3. NUCLEAR ASSAULT – Handle with Care
4. EXODUS – Bonded by Blood
5. NAILS – Unsilent Death

6. NACHTMYSTIUM – Silencing Machine
7. IRON MAIDEN – Killers
8. GOJIRA – From Mars to Sirius
9. GHOST – Opus Eponymous
10. FEAR FACTORY – Demanufacture

*Can't lie—there was also some Bad Brains, Agnostic Front, Cro-Mags, and Leeway thrown in for good measure.

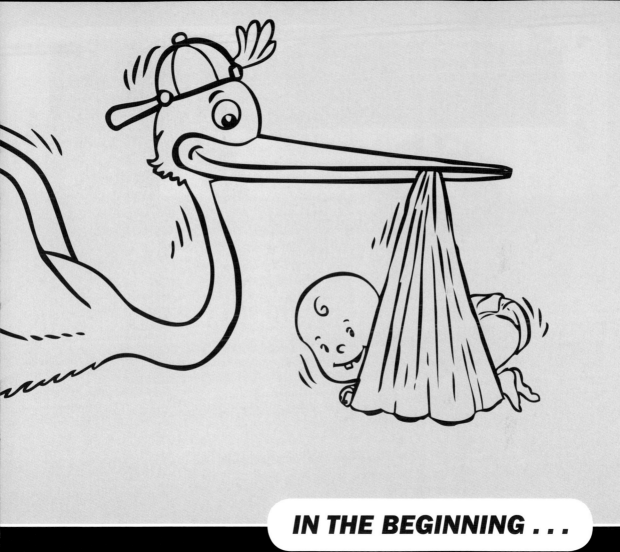

IN THE BEGINNING . . .

MOST IMPORTANT METAL DEMOS OF ALL TIME
Compiled by Monte Conner, Borivoj Krgin, and Shaun Glass

These are some of the most sought after, influential, and overall noteworthy demos to surface in the early trading days, compiled by three people who know their shit when it comes to xeroxed covers and double cassette tape decks.

1. METALLICA – NO LIFE 'TIL LEATHER
2. NASTY SAVAGE – WAGE OF MAYHEM
3. DEATH – EARLY DEMOS
4. OVERKILL – POWER IN BLACK
5. MEGADETH – EARLY DEMOS
6. MORBID ANGEL – THY KINGDOM COME
7. MEDIEVAL – ALL KNOBS TO THE RIGHT
8. LEGACY – DEMO:1
9. ANVIL CHORUS
10. VIO-LENCE
11. ZOETROPE – METAL LOG VOL. 1
12. SODOM
13. FORBIDDEN EVIL
14. MASTER – '85 DEMO
15. DEATH STRIKE – FUCKIN' DEATH

TOP 10 DEMO TAPE TRADERS: "FROM TAPE TRADERS TO GAME CHANGERS" *by ILL BILL*

We owe these folks a lot.

1. LARS ULRICH
2. BRIAN SLAGEL
3. RON QUINTANA
4. BOB MULDOWNEY
5. JON ZAZULA
6. BOB NALBANDIAN
7. BERNARD DOE
8. CHUCK SCHULDINER
9. BORIVOJ KRGIN
10. MONTE CONNER

TOP 20 HEAVY METAL FANZINES OF ALL TIME by ILL BILL

Our CNN, NPR, *60 Minutes,* and *The Onion* all rolled into one.

1. METAL MANIA (Ron Quintana)
2. THE NEW HEAVY METAL REVUE (Brian Slagel)
3. KICK ASS MONTHLY (Bob Muldowney)
4. HEADBANGER (Bob Nalbandian)
5. METAL FORCES (Bernard Doe)
6. VIOLENT NOIZE (Borivoj Krgin)
7. THE WILD RAG! (Richard C)
8. SLAYER (Metalion)
9. ULTIMATUM (Kim August)
10. INVINCIBLE FORCE (Bryan Daniel)
11. THE BOOK OF ARMAGEDDON (Ed Farshtey)
12. METAL MELTDOWN (Jeff VanderClute)
13. PEARDROP ZINE (Laurent Merle)
14. CEREBRAL HOLOCAUST (Paul Zimmerman)
15. NO GLAM FAGS (Marco Barbieri)
16. METAL FRONTLINE (Will Tarrent)
17. F.E.T.U. (zine based out of Japan)
18. SACROFORMITY (Jacob Hansen)
19. RIPPING HEADACHES (Bruce Davis)
20. UNI-FORCE (Mark Sawickis)

IMPENDING
DOOM....

HOLY MOSES ★ EXCALIBUR ★ WRECKING CREW ★
OVERDOSE ★ SODOM ★ MUCKY PUP ★ BELGIAN A. ★

Mercyful Fate • Fear Factory • Marduk
Genitorturers • Pariah • Angel Corpse

METAL MANIA

$1.00

Merciless metallic Mayhem

#9

IRON
MAIDEN
ACCEPT
RAVEN
METALLICA
MERCYFUL
FATE

MOTORHEAD
EXCITER
MEGADETH
VOI VOD
MEDIEVAL
ZOETROPE
BLACK LACE

photo by Frank White

The Book of Armageddon

ISSUE
#-
$2.

DARK
ANGEL
CELTIC FROST
DEATH

BATHORY
POSSESSED
DESECRATION

INSIDE - INTERVIEWS,
SHOW REVIEWS, ALBUM
+ TAPE REVIEWS + MUCH
MORE

HEAD BANGER

Chastain

foto: Banger Bart.

no: 11 f 2,50

GRIFFIN
DEATH

SLAYER

ALBUMS: THE GOOD, THE BAD, AND THE REALLY UGLY

THE BEST METAL ALBUMS <u>EVER</u>!

1. BLACK SABBATH – S/T (1970)
2. IRON MAIDEN – The Number of the Beast (1982)
3. SLAYER – Reign in Blood (1986)
4. METALLICA – Ride the Lightning (1984)
5. MOTÖRHEAD – No Sleep 'til Hammersmith (1981)
6. JUDAS PRIEST – British Steel (1980)
7. IRON MAIDEN – Killers (1981)
8. EXODUS – Bonded by Blood (1985)
9. SEPULTURA – Beneath the Remains (1989)
10. VENOM – Black Metal (1982)
11. CELTIC FROST – Morbid Tales (1984)
12. METALLICA – Master of Puppets (1986)
13. NUCLEAR ASSAULT – Survive (1988)
14. FEAR FACTORY – Demanufacture (1995)
15. MANOWAR – Battle Hymns (1982)
16. MERCYFUL FATE – Don't Break the Oath (1984)
17. ANTHRAX – Spreading the Disease (1985)
18. VOIVOD – Killing Technology (1987)
19. MÖTLEY CRÜE – Too Fast for Love (1981)
20. SLAYER – Hell Awaits (1985)

10 REASONS WHY <u>EVERYONE</u> LOVES SLAYER'S REIGN IN BLOOD

There's no need for any setup on this one. The list says it all.

1. Any album played at an average of 210 BPM is awesome.

2. The album features probably the greatest collection of riffs ever played on one album.

3. Tom Araya's voice is the most perfect combination of clarity and anger ever captured in a recording.

4. The fact that *Reign* came out on Def Jam is just friggin' incredible.

5. "Angel of Death," while being one of the greatest Metal songs of all time, has an extremely high freak-your-parents-out factor.

6. Every single note on the album was written by a member of Slayer.

7. While most Thrash Metal bands at that time were slowing down, in search of "commercial success" on their third albums, Slayer played even faster and got big anyway.

8. *Reign in Blood* was the first Slayer album to feature artwork by then political illustrator Larry Carroll, who created imagery as brutal and concise as the album's music.

9. When played live, the songs from *Reign in Blood* have incited countless injuries, as well as minor and major violence.

10. Is there really any better way to spend twenty-nine minutes???

KILL 'EM ALL VS. RIDE THE LIGHTNING VS. MASTER OF PUPPETS VS. . . . AND JUSTICE FOR ALL

by Flemming Rasmussen

If you're one of "us"—who scans album credits as if our lives depended on it—you know that Flemming Rasmussen is responsible for producing three of the most amazing and important Metal albums of all time. For all intents and purposes, he was Metallica band member number 5 during their "glory years," including the time of their seemingly impossible transition from Cliff Burton to Jason Newsted on bass, and helped shape the sound and production value of Heavy Metal forever. The sound, the playing, etc., varies substantially from album to album, simply because of evolution alone, but stylistically, each has a very distinct personality. Here are a few thoughts from Flemming as to what he believes each of the three albums improves upon its predecessor.

Ride the Lightning vs. Kill 'Em All

1. The drum sound on *Ride* is much better than on *Kill*.
2. Although we tried to emulate the guitar sound of *Kill 'Em All*, it got a lot better on *Ride the Lightning*.
3. Lars's drumming improved 200 percent on *Ride*.
4. Cliff was brilliant on *Ride*.
5. Overall band performance is much better on *Ride the Lightning*.

Master of Puppets vs. Ride the Lightning

1. The "Metallica Thrash Sound" is perfected on *Master of Puppets*.
2. Everybody performed better.
3. Songwriting is generally better on *Master*.
4. James's guitar picking was world-class on *Master*.
5. The food during the session was better (my wife cooked for us!).

. . . And Justice for All vs. Master of Puppets

1. Kirk's solo at the end of "One" is a masterpiece.
2. Lars's drumming improved even more on *. . . And Justice for All*.
3. Everybody was playing tighter, and the guitar sound is GREAT.
4. We went from 12 [hours] to 14–16 hours of work a day.
5. Album sales!

The melding of hardcore with Metal in the mid-'80s was both a blessing (for hardcore) and a curse (for hardcore). While it resuscitated the movement from the painful musical stagnation it was experiencing, it destroyed the ethics of the scene. Every hesher in America grasped on to hardcore as their street-cred security blanket and, in many cases, made the whole thing downright goofy. That said, some great music came from this mash-up, and here are some of the best examples:

1. D.R.I. – Dealing with It!
2. LEEWAY – Born to Expire
3. CORROSION OF CONFORMITY – Animosity
4. AGNOSTIC FRONT – Cause for Alarm
5. SUICIDAL TENDENCIES – S/T
6. CRUMBSUCKERS – Life of Dreams
7. EXCEL – Split Image
8. DISCHARGE – Hear Nothing See Nothing Say Nothing
9. CRO-MAGS – The Age of Quarrel
10. VENOM – Welcome to Hell
11. SICK OF IT ALL – Just Look Around
12. KILLING TIME – Brightside
13. BIOHAZARD – Urban Discipline
14. VISION OF DISORDER – Imprint
15. LUDICHRIST – Immaculate Deception
16. BAD BRAINS – Quickness
17. THE ACCÜSED – The Return of Martha Splatterhead
18. ATTITUDE ADJUSTMENT – American Paranoia
19. S.O.D. – Speak English or Die
20. CRYPTIC SLAUGHTER – Convicted
21. PRONG – Force Fed
22. CARNIVORE – S/T
23. JUDGE – Bringin' It Down
24. MADBALL – Legacy
25. BROKEN BONES – Dem Bones

It's no secret that Thrash did not originate with Metal, but with hardcore. The speed and energy of superfast punk bands—which ultimately helped create what eventually became known as hardcore—was musically unprecedented, and the way that energy affected a crowd of angry kids bordered on the dangerous. When Metal bands began to unearth these groups and apply their high-BPM chaos to the quickly becoming stale Maiden/Priest vibe of the early 1980s, it was on, and it changed Metal forever. Here are some of the albums that the early Thrash Metal bands heard and were clearly influenced by:

1. DISCHARGE – HEAR NOTHING SEE NOTHING SAY NOTHING (1982)

2. D.R.I. – DIRTY ROTTEN LP (1983)

3. CORROSION OF CONFORMITY – EYE FOR AN EYE (1984)

4. CHARGED G.B.H. – CITY BABY ATTACKED BY RATS (1982)

5. BROKEN BONES – DEM BONES (1984)

6. SEPTIC DEATH – NEED SO MUCH ATTENTION (1984)

7. BLACK FLAG – DAMAGED (1981)

8. AGNOSTIC FRONT – VICTIM IN PAIN (1984)

9. MINOR THREAT – S/T (1981)

10. BAD BRAINS – S/T (ROIR CASSETTE, 1982)

5 SHARK-JUMPING RECORDINGS

A lot of folks really don't know where the expression "jumping the shark" comes from. Its birth can be traced back to an ill-fated 1977 episode of the hit sitcom *Happy Days*, where Fonzie, the long-standing poster boy for "cool," actually jumped over a shark on water skis. The show never recovered, and the term has come to represent "the point of no return" for pretty much everything. Metal albums are no exception, and these vinyl pieces of disappointment are proof.

1. **DEF LEPPARD, PYROMANIA** – Def Lep was pretty much a NWOBHM (New Wave of British Heavy Metal) band until this turd dropped from pop music's ass.

2. **CELTIC FROST, COLD LAKE** – *Into the Pandemonium* is still great, but this Swiss nightmare is inexcusable.

3. **IRON MAIDEN, SOMEWHERE IN TIME** – We're down for "progressing" and everything, but this marks the point where Maiden stopped sounding like Maiden.

4. **ANTHRAX, I'M THE MAN** – The fine line between pioneering and EMBARRASSING! Scott was always pretty open about his love for hip-hop, but this was NOT dope!

5. **METALLICA, LOAD/RELOAD** – Flogging this dead horse is completely unnecessary. However, if you're one of those deranged people who hates the Black Album, you're just a HATER!!!

THE VERY **BEST** QUALITIES OF METALLICA'S LOAD AND RELOAD ALBUMS

The Merciless Book of Metal Lists

Nuff said.

200 EMBARRASSINGLY BAD ALBUM COVERS

We don't care what your band name is, or what stage of your career it may be—there's got to be a way to express your artistic vision without it looking like your (epileptic) six-year-old niece created your cover art with boogers and doodie. Here are two hundred of the absolute-worst album covers we have seen, anywhere . . . **EVER**.

1. **ANTHRAX – Fistful of Metal**

2. ANTHRAX – State of Euphoria
3. MEGADETH – Killing Is My Business

4. **ACCEPT – Balls to the Wall**

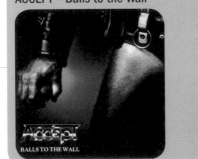

5. METALLICA – Load
6. IRON CROSS – Too Hot to Rock

7. VINNIE VINCENT INVASION – S/T
8. KROKUS – The Blitz
9. KNORKATOR – Hasenchartbreaker
10. DRAGONFORCE – Ultra Beatdown
11. ACID REIGN – Moshkinstein
12. NME – Unholy Death
13. ROGUE MALE – First Visit
14. PANTERA – Projects in the Jungle
15. PANTERA – Metal Magic
16. CINDERELLA – Night Songs
17. FASTWAY – Trick or Treat
18. KINGPIN – Welcome to Bop City
19. AUTOPSY – ShitFun
20. CATTLE DECAPITATION – Humanure
21. HOLY TERROR – Terror and Submission
22. DREAM THEATER – When Dream and Day Unite

23. **WHIPLASH – Power and Pain**

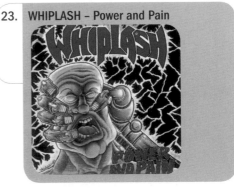

24. METAL SKOOL – S/T
25. PRETTY BOY FLOYD – Leather Boyz with Electric Toyz
26. **RAVEN – Stay Hard**

27. RAVEN – The Pack Is Back
28. RAVEN – Life's a Bitch
29. **RAVEN – Nothing Exceeds Like Excess**

30. THE ACCÜSED – The Curse of Martha Splatterhead
31. GWAR – Lust in Space
32. HALLOWS EVE – Tales of Terror
33. TANKARD – The Beauty and the Beer
34. DEVOURMENT – Molesting the Decapitated
35. SAMSON – Last Rites
36. SAMSON – Thank You and Goodnight
37. E-X-E – Stricken by Might
38. MACE – Process of Elimination
39. MACE – The Evil in Good

40. **WRATHCHILD – Stakk Attakk**

41. IMMORTAL – Battles in the North
42. PANDEMONIUM – The Kill
43. RIOT – Thundersteel
44. MADAM X – We Reserve the Right
45. PAT BOONE – In a Metal Mood
46. RIOT – Narita
47. SACRED RITE – S/T
48. SADUS – Illusions
49. M.O.D. – Surfin' M.O.D.
50. DEF LEPPARD – High 'n' Dry
51. KILLER DWARFS – Big Deal
52. WINGER – S/T
53. LIMP BIZKIT – Gold Cobra

54. **MANOWAR – Into Glory Ride**

55. MANOWAR – Anthology
56. STRYPER – To Hell with the Devil

57. SEPULTURA – Morbid Visions
58. SEPULTURA – Bestial Devastation
59. PUNGENT STENCH – Been Caught Buttering
60. DESTRUCTION – Sentence of Death
61. RAGE – Execution Guaranteed
62. W.A.S.P. – Inside the Electric Circus

63. **WHIPLASH – Insult to Injury**

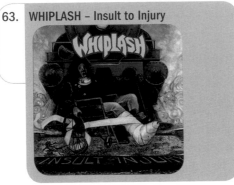

64. WHIPLASH – Thrashback
65. BATTLEAXE – Burn This Town
66. THE GREAT KAT – Bloody Vivaldi
67. BONDED BY BLOOD – Extinguish the Weak
68. YNGWIE J. MALMSTEEN – Trilogy
69. KING KOBRA – Thrill of a Lifetime
70. HIGH TENSION – Masters of Madness
71. TOMMY LEE – Tommyland: The Ride
72. EXCITER – Violence & Force

73. **MERCILESS DEATH – Evil in the Night**

74. HELLOWEEN – Chameleon
75. HELLOWEEN – Keeper of the Seven Keys, Part 1

76. **DEVIN TOWNSEND – Infinity**

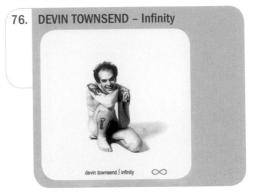

77. OBITUARY – Slowly We Rot
78. FIREAXE – Victory or Death
79. VICE – Made for Pleasure
80. ACID BATH – When the Kite String Pops
81. RUNNING WILD – Masquerade
82. RUNNING WILD – Port Royal
83. RUNNING WILD – Black Hand Inn
84. METAL CHURCH – Hanging in the Balance
85. METAL CHURCH – The Human Factor

86. **VIO-LENCE – Eternal Nightmare**

87. SAVATAGE – Gutter Ballet
88. CARCASS – Swansong
89. CRUMBSUCKERS – B.O.M.B.

90. ICED EARTH – The Dark Saga
91. SODOM – Get What You Deserve
92. ATTACKER – Battle at Helms Deep
93. WRATHCHILD AMERICA – Climbin' the Walls

94. **THE RODS – Let Them Eat Metal**

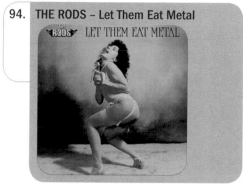

95. CITIES – Annihilation Absolute
96. TT QUICK – Sloppy Seconds
97. NUCLEAR ASSAULT – Something Wicked
98. METALWOLF – Down to the Wire

99. **MIDNIGHT CHASER – Rough and Tough**

100. HELLMOUTH – Gravestone Skylines
101. CANNIBAL CORPSE – Eaten Back to Life
102. VIRGIN STEELE – Age of Consent
103. VIRGIN STEELE – Life Among the Ruins
104. ANTHRAX – We've Come for You All
105. WHITESNAKE – Lovehunter

106. SAXON – S/T
107. TWISTED SISTER – Stay Hungry
108. BONED – Up at the Crack
109. KEVIN DUBROW – In for the Kill
110. FIST – Back with a Vengeance

111. **AGRESSOR – Neverending Destiny**

112. ELIMINATOR – Breaking the Wheel
113. MELIAH RAGE – Kill to Survive
114. MELIAH RAGE – Masquerade
115. MELIAH RAGE – Unfinished Business
116. MELIAH RAGE – Barely Human
117. SAVAGE THRUST – Eat 'Em Raw
118. SAVAGE GRACE – The Dominatress
119. SAVAGE GRACE – Master of Disguise
120. JON MIKL THOR – Recruits (Wild in the Streets)

121. **HALLOWS EVE – The Neverending Sleep**

122. BARN BURNER – Bangers
123. STRYKEN – First Strike
124. BATTLECROSS – Pursuit of Honor
125. ANCIENT – Mad Grandiose Bloodfiends
126. GWAR – Bloody Pit of Horror
127. METAL MASSACRE COMPILATION – VOL I
128. METAL MASSACRE COMPILATION – VOL II
129. METAL MASSACRE COMPILATION – VOL III
130. METAL MASSACRE COMPILATION – VOL IV
131. METAL MASSACRE COMPILATION – VOL V

132. METAL MASSACRE COMPILATION – VOL VI

133. METAL MASSACRE COMPILATION – VOL VII
134. METAL MASSACRE COMPILATION – VOL VIII
135. METAL MASSACRE COMPILATION – VOL X
136. METAL MASSACRE COMPILATION – VOL XI
137. METAL MASSACRE COMPILATION – VOL XII

138. RAVAGE – The End of Tomorrow

139. PENTAGRAM – When the Screams Come
140. WEHRMACHT – Shark Attack
141. FUELED BY FIRE – Plunging into Darkness

142. FUELED BY FIRE – Spread the Fire

143. HATCHET – Awaiting Evil
144. BLOODLUST – Guilty as Sin
145. IRON FIRE – Voyage of the Damned
146. CAULDRON – Chained to the Nite
147. LIZZY BORDEN – Menace to Society
148. ALL THAT REMAINS – The Fall of Ideals
149. RAZOR – Violent Restitution
150. OMEN – The Curse
151. JAGUAR – Power Games
152. TANK – Filth Hounds of Hades
153. THUNDERSTICK – Beauty and the Beasts
154. THUNDERSTICK – Echoes from the Analogue Asylum

155. SAMSON – Head On

156. CHARIOT – Burning Ambition
157. HAWAII – S/T
158. OZ – Fire in the Brain
159. WARFARE – A Conflict of Hatred
160. WARFARE – Metal Anarchy
161. GRIM REAPER – Fear No Evil
162. BROCAS HELM – Defender of the Crown
163. ANGEL WITCH – Screamin' n' Bleedin'

164. ATOMKRAFT – Future Warriors

165. ATOMKRAFT – Queen of Death
166. SKULL FIST – Heavier Than Metal
167. 220 VOLT – Mind Over Muscle
168. 100% PROOF – S/T
169. BRUCE DICKINSON – Tyranny of Souls

170. BRUCE DICKINSON – Balls to Picasso

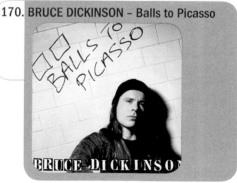

171. BRUCE DICKINSON – Accident of Birth
172. BLAZE BAYLEY – The Night That Will Not Die
173. ENFORCER – Diamonds

174. DAVID "ROCK" FEINSTEIN – One Night in the Jungle
175. CAULDRON – Into the Cauldron
176. BITCH – Be My Slave
177. CLOVEN HOOF – S/T
178. CLOVEN HOOF – Throne of Damnation
179. BLACK TEARS – Child of the Storm
180. BLACK RAVEN – The Day of the Raven

181. AXEWITCH – Pray for Metal

182. CHAINSAW – Massacre
183. CRONOS – Dancing in the Fire
184. EZY MEAT – Rock Your Brains
185. EZY MEAT – Not for Wimps
186. KROKUS – Pay It in Metal
187. ANNIHILATOR – Criteria for a Black Widow
188. JAG PANZER – Tyrants
189. GIRLSCHOOL – Take a Bite
190. GIRLSCHOOL – Demolition
191. MARSHALL LAW – Metal Detector
192. CHROME MOLLY – You Can't Have It All
193. CHROME MOLLY – Stick It Out
194. GRAVE DIGGER – War Games
195. SINNER – Touch of Sin
196. SINNER – Dangerous Charm
197. SINNER – Danger Zone
198. DEMON – Hold On to the Dream
199. GRAND PRIX – S/T
200. TYGERS OF PAN TANG – Burning in the Shade

AXES BOLD AS FUCK

30 OF THE GREATEST METAL GUITARISTS

When it comes to Heavy Metal, or even rock for that matter, there is no topic more vivaciously debated than "Who is the best guitarist?" More often than not, the answer is Eddie Van Halen, but even a head of lettuce knows Eddie just ain't Metal! The axe is clearly the instrument that defines the Metal genre, and here is a collection of its premier gunslingers:

1. TONY IOMMI – Black Sabbath
2. ADRIAN SMITH/DAVE MURRAY – Iron Maiden
3. GLENN TIPTON AND K.K. DOWNING – Judas Priest
4. KERRY KING AND JEFF HANNEMAN – Slayer
5. JAMES HETFIELD AND KIRK HAMMETT – Metallica
6. YNGWIE MALMSTEEN
7. RANDY RHOADS – Ozzy Osbourne
8. DIMEBAG DARRELL – Pantera/Damageplan
9. DAVE MUSTAINE – Megadeth
10. DEVIN TOWNSEND – Strapping Young Lad/Devin Townsend Project
11. GARY HOLT AND RICK HUNOLT – Exodus

20 OF THE GREATEST METAL BASS PLAYERS

Bassists are probably the most underappreciated members of any band. Without them, you don't FEEL the band; there is neither a bottom end nor rhythmic cohesiveness. Listen to Metallica's . . . *And Justice for All* or any Pantera album and tell us we're wrong. Here are twenty REAL gods of thunder:

1. GEEZER BUTLER – Black Sabbath
2. STEVE HARRIS – Iron Maiden
3. CLIFF BURTON – Metallica
4. DANNY LILKER – Nuclear Assault/S.O.D.
5. DAVE ELLEFSON – Megadeth
6. RYAN MARTINIE – Mudvayne
7. IAN HILL – Judas Priest
8. JOEY DeMAIO – Manowar
9. GREG CHRISTIAN – Testament
10. TOM ARAYA – Slayer
11. JASON NEWSTED – Metallica
12. ROB TRUJILLO – Metallica/Suicidal Tendencies
13. LEMMY – Motörhead
14. CHRISTIAN OLDE WOLBERS – Fear Factory
15. ADRIAN LAMBERT – DragonForce
16. TIM HANSEN – Mercyful Fate/King Diamond
17. PETER STEELE – Carnivore/Type O Negative
18. JEFF BECERRA – Possessed
19. FRANK BELLO – Anthrax
20. JOHN CAMPBELL – Lamb of God

I have never played an instrument, save for a brief stint with the clarinet in first grade (Howie speaking here), but I am hyper-aware of one's ability to play and, equally important, the tone blaring from a player's rig. Without any technical knowledge of gear, it is obvious when a guitarist or bassist has crafted a tone that can move you, scare the shit out of you, or maybe even KILL you. So many early Metal albums had tiny production budgets and did not come close to replicating the fury that the best bands unleash live. Therefore, we want to highlight a handful of the very best axe players whose tones, either recorded or otherwise, assault the ears and souls of Heads for all you Guitar Center–obsessed, bedroom guitar masturbators to try and emulate for your band.

BEST GUITAR TONES

TONY IOMMI – The man set the bar high from day one. His sound drips with darkness and evil and POWER. While we're sure his setup was pretty primitive back when he laid it down on Sabbath's early albums, his style, settings, and maybe even his lack of fingertips created a monster of beautifully grand proportions and literally set the Heavy Metal tone forever.

JAMES HETFIELD – If Iommi brought the evil, Hetfield supplied the crunch. His rhythm sound is the standard for modern Metal and all of its offshoots. The picking style popularized in the Bay Area has a lot to do with it, and James is its best ambassador. While it was strong on *Kill 'Em All*, by the time *Ride the Lightning* hit the earwaves, Hetfield had set the new standard by bringing a guitar sound capable of crumbling a city.

SCOTT IAN – Very similar story to that of James Hetfield. Ian's tone is huge. However, it was often crushed by the production of Anthrax's albums. If you listen to *Spreading the Disease*, there's a massive rhythm sound underneath all the layers of EQ and "production value." Scott thankfully had his live shit together, and he could move a room with the best of them.

DINO CAZARES – Fast-forward a few years to the '90s, and Fear Factory's Dino Cazares found a whole new way to slaughter you with his thick, murderous tone. He is super-precise as a player, and his sound flies out of his rig with an intensity that's rare in latter-day Metal.

GREG FULTON – One of the most slept-on dudes in the game. There's a reason Chicago's Znowhite were underground royalty, and that reason is Greg. He may actually have come closest to replicating Hetfield's glorious noise, and watching this mountain of a man deliver the goods up close and personal was always amazing!

BEST BASS TONES

GEEZER BUTLER – Geezer is every bit the bassist that Iommi is a guitar player. He isn't flashy, but that low-end rumble can make you lose your lunch from note one. Plus, he plays without a pick, which keeps it heavy at all times.

LEMMY – His tone is legendary, and honestly, his ultra-distorted Rickenbacker basically serves as an additional guitar for Motörhead and is crucial to their sound. Technically, Lemmy's tone is a 7. From a homicidal power perspective—easily an 11.

DANNY LILKER – If there had never been any guitarists in Danny's bands, he could still kill a venue packed with kids. He kept his tone a true bass tone, but it was always distorted just enough to have a personality of its own. Totally instrumental in shaping the overall sound of Anthrax, Nuclear Assault, and, of course, S.O.D.

CRONOS – Clearly not the "best" bassist, but his tone was over-the-fucking-top and incredibly influential. It evoked images of Satan himself with every thunderous note, and made you wince if you were too close to the PA bins. Did I say "wince"? I meant "vomit"!

TOM ARAYA – Another guy who isn't the most technical, but whose tone is monumentally influential. Tom's bass sounds like a bass. It is bottom heavy and perfectly moves every song along with Kerry and Jeff's guitar work, matching and complementing the insane explosiveness that is Slayer.

SCREAM FOR ME

20 OF THE GREATEST METAL VOICES

One of the best things about Metal is the diversity of the vocals from band to band. To us, Lemmy is every bit as great as Bruce Dickinson. Vocal style is ultimately determined by what the music requires. Look at Iron Maiden for instance. Paul Di'Anno made the band great, while Bruce took them into the stratosphere. We love both, and both will always represent Iron Maiden as far as most are concerned. Check out some of the top vocalists and frontmen below:

1. RONNIE JAMES DIO – Black Sabbath/Dio
2. ROB HALFORD – Judas Priest
3. BRUCE DICKINSON – Iron Maiden
4. ERIC ADAMS – Manowar
5. GEOFF TATE – Queensrÿche
6. KING DIAMOND – Mercyful Fate/King Diamond
7. TOM ARAYA – Slayer
8. JOHN BUSH – Armored Saint/Anthrax
9. JAMES HETFIELD – Metallica
10. MAX CAVALERA – Sepultura/Soulfly
11. PAUL BALOFF – Exodus
12. LEMMY – Motörhead
13. SNAKE – Voivod
14. COREY TAYLOR – Slipknot
15. TOM G. WARRIOR – Celtic Frost
16. UDO DIRKSCHNEIDER – Accept/U.D.O.
17. TIM "RIPPER" OWENS – Judas Priest
18. CRONOS – Venom
19. OZZY OSBOURNE – Black Sabbath/Ozzy
20. PETER STEELE – Carnivore/Type O Negative

ROB HALFORD'S LYRICS RE-EXAMINED

Judas Priest is one of the finest and most influential bands of all time. The amazing Rob Halford walked it like he talked it, and young men everywhere worshipped his every word (at face value). When he announced to the world in 1998 that he was gay, it was safe to assume that nasty, homophobic tirades would fly from everywhere, but we were pleasantly surprised when the Metal world, by and large, accepted Rob for exactly who he was and showed him the respect he had earned many times over. With that, you can't help but think how uncomfortable this announcement must have made a number of Priest's early followers, when it came to Rob's lyrics. Imagine, if you will, being an awkward teenage boy screaming along to every single thing shrieked by Halford at a Priest show back in the day . . . Fist in the air, chest puffed out, oblivious to the rest of the universe. Priest RULES, and you have become a slave to every riff, each delivered vocal, and all of the ill-advised choreography—only to find out "Hell Bent for Leather" doesn't mean exactly what you thought it did. Rob had PENIS on his mind, but no one was publicly aware of his love for the skin flute as of yet! So, we think it wise to take a closer look at some of what Robbie boy had to say throughout the years and explore what he REALLY meant:

1. **"YOU'VE GOT ANOTHER THING COMIN'"**
   I'm callin' all the shots / I got an ace card comin' down on the rocks

   Rob's like, "Shut up bitch—I'm the top here, and I'm gonna pound you until my load drips down your balls!"

2. **"BREAKING THE LAW"**
   Nobody cares if I live or die / So I might as well begin to put some action in my life

   Obviously Rob feels alienated because his friends refuse to accept his lifestyle, so he hops a bus to San Francisco to get laid.

3. **"LIVING AFTER MIDNIGHT"**
   I'm all geared up to score again, loaded, loaded / I come alive in the neon light

   Rob seems to not have gotten any in a while, so during a visit to Amsterdam, he hits the Red Light District in search of a Dutch stallion.

4. **"HOT FOR LOVE"**
   I can't shake you off / You're a wolf on the prowl

   As he stated in "You've Got Another Thing Comin'," Rob fancies himself a pitcher, although as evidenced by this here passage, he doesn't necessarily mind role-playing as Yogi Berra now and again.

5. **"ROCK HARD RIDE FREE"**
   Get a grip on the action / Moving heaven and earth

   Really . . . Who DOESN'T like some nice hand release???

6. **"SOME HEADS ARE GONNA ROLL"**
   If the man with the power / Can't keep it under control / Some heads are gonna roll

   If this isn't the perfect slogan for premature ejaculators, we don't know what is!

7. **"NEW BEGINNINGS"**
   A new beginning has arrived / At the crossroads of my life / This new love keeps me alive

   Finally, Rob Halford finds himself free from the shackles of discrimination and prejudice. Homophobia is fucked up and wrong. All due respect to a true Metal pioneer.

GLORIOUS PAUL BALOFF STAGE BANTER

The tragically deceased, but truly unforgettable Paul Baloff left us with one of the greatest Metal albums of all time—the mighty Exodus' *Bonded by Blood*, as well as some blazing shows. And from those shows come a number of the greatest quotes to ever leave the mouth of a Metal frontman. Exodus gigs, while Paul was in the band, were like a game of "I can't wait to hear what the hell he's going to say next" in the most fantastic way. I miss Paul and hope he is resting easy . . . and killing every fucking poser he encounters in Metal heaven. Batch number one is from Exodus gunslinger and founding member Gary Holt, and the others are unforgettable bits too spectacular to keep to ourselves.

"Yeeeeeeeeeeeaaaaaaaaaaaahhhhhhhhhhhh!!!"
—Paul Baloff

Part I by Gary Holt

"Smash everything, leave nothing unsmashed!"

"This ain't no Arsenio Hall show, destroy something!"

"Talk minus action equals nothing!"

"Randy, get 'Muh' outta here!"

"Hold in your pee, don't pee yet, you get drunker when you hold in your pee!"

"This song is older than shit, heavier than time!"

"My grandmother screams louder than you, and she's DEAD!"

"Thanks to Gary and Tom and Jack and Rick for letting me be so heavy!"

"Heavy must stay together, all others must die!"

*"I don't get tired until the songs are over, then I just simply **die**!"*

Part II

"This next song, it ain't about no goldfish, and it ain't about no tuna fish, and it ain't about no trout . . . this song is called 'Piranha'!" – **Said at every Exodus show since the song was written**

"I wanna know how many of you people go out in the streets looking to kick someone's fucking ass . . . maybe a couple of posers, you know . . . head on down to the local disco and hang out and waste a couple of people." – **The Combat Tour, NYC, April 1985**

"KILL!!!" – **Dynamo Club, Eindhoven, Holland, October 1985**

"You know what I think about posers, it's already been said, if you see one—KILL IT!"
– **Piranha show, Stockton, CA, September 1990**

"You guys just fucking rule! I said that shit last night, and last night they did fucking rule, but tonight, you fucking rule. You're just one-upping this shit all the way to hell." – **Albany, NY, 1997**

"This one's about violence . . . it's fucking everywhere . . . it's part of your lives, whether you like it or not, so you might as well get good at it!" – **Dynamo Open Air, Eindhoven, Holland, Summer 1997**

"I'm not gonna say anything about posers being killed, but personally I just can't help myself. This is where all posers belong . . . They belong on [along with the crowd] 'Death Row'!"
– **The Stone, San Francisco, 1985**

"We're gonna do one last song for ya. It's about a rather nice guy who lived in the seventeenth century. He got mad at his citizens, and he impaled twenty-five thousand of them on poles. What a nice guy. His name was Vladimir, and he was called Vlad the Impaler."
– **Dynamo Club, Eindhoven, Holland, 1985**

"This is the most Metal fuckers I've ever played for in my entire fucking life, man. You guys fucking rule . . . everyone else should fucking die!" – **Dynamo Open Air, Eindhoven, Holland, Summer 1997**

"You guys look like you're just ready to kill anyone who gets in your fucking way right now!"
– **CBGB, NYC, Summer 1997**

10 ACCOMPLISHMENTS IRON MAIDEN WOULD NEVER HAVE ACHIEVED HAD PAUL DI'ANNO REMAINED THEIR SINGER

We've loved Maiden since their debut first found its way to our ears, and *Killers* is awesome too, but c'mon—had Bruce Dickinson remained in the painfully mediocre Samson, none of this stuff would have happened:

1. They never would have released arguably the greatest Heavy Metal album of all time—*The Number of the Beast*.

2. They would never have had a mostly sober, drug-free singer.

3. They would not have had a number-one album (let alone many of them) anywhere in the world.

4. They would never have been afforded the opportunity of having Bruce Dickinson fly them and the crew around the world for the Somewhere Back in Time and Final Frontier tours in their own jet.

5. They definitely wouldn't have won a Grammy.

6. The song "The Number of the Beast" surely would not have had the unbelievable scream it features at 1:18 into the track.

7. They probably would not have allowed Adrian Smith's "temporary" replacement, Janick Gers, to overstay his welcome if Paul was still front and center (wimps!).

8. The band would never have become as universally synonymous with "Satan" as they have.

9. They sure as hell couldn't have had an all-female tribute band called the "Iron Maidens" performing in their honor.

10. They just never would have gotten "BIG!"

POUNDING METAL

25 OF THE GREATEST METAL DRUMMERS

The power of Heavy Metal drums just cannot be understated. While some people were marveling at the rhythmic wizardry of guys like Neil Peart, we were caught up in the power and the glory of the hardest-hitting, most intense skin bashers to ever take the throne behind a kit. Each of these twenty-five would make Animal from the Muppets incredibly proud.

1. DAVE LOMBARDO – Slayer
2. BILL WARD – Black Sabbath
3. CHARLIE BENANTE – Anthrax/S.O.D.
4. NICKO MCBRAIN – Iron Maiden
5. GENE HOGLAN – Dark Angel/Strapping Young Lad
6. VINNIE PAUL – Pantera/Damageplan
7. IGOR CAVALERA – Sepultura
8. MATT MCDONOUGH – Mudvayne
9. MARIO DUPLANTIER – Gojira
10. RAYMOND HERRERA – Fear Factory
11. PHIL "PHILTHY ANIMAL" TAYLOR – Motörhead
12. LOUIE CLEMENTE – Testament
13. ROY MAYORGA – Soulfly/Stone Sour
14. TOM HUNTING – Exodus
15. MIKE PORTNOY – Dream Theater
16. MIKE BORDIN – Ozzy Osbourne
17. TOMMY LEE – Mötley Crüe
18. DAN BEEHLER – Exciter
19. SCOTT COLUMBUS – Manowar
20. VINNY APPICE – Dio/Heaven & Hell
21. RICHARD CHRISTY – Death/Iced Earth/Charred Walls of the Damned
22. MIKE SUS – Possessed
23. JÜRGEN REIL – Kreator
24. JOEY JORDISON – Slipknot
25. CHRIS KONTOS – Machine Head

STUPID, STUPID, STUPID

COMPLETELY UNNECESSARY HEAVY METAL SUBGENRES

One of the dumbest developments over the years when it comes to Metal is the "creation" of all these subgenres. It was all just "Metal" until someone decided they didn't want to be associated with certain other bands, so they took it upon themselves and created a new "thing" in order to feel special. Making great music should be enough, and no band should ever feel the need to "explain" itself, but somewhere between overly self-conscious band members and self-absorbed journalists lies this silliness:

1. **MATH METAL** – Yay! You play challenging time signatures and spend hours screwing around in Guitar Center after school. Yay!
2. **POST-METAL** – If you're so proud of being considered as such, please remove the name "Metal" altogether and move forward with your pompous, "I'm too intelligent and experimental to be Metal" bullshit.
3. **TEUTONIC THRASH METAL** – Sooooo, this just means you're from Germany and like Slayer?
4. **NSBM** – Black Metal for those who dig *Mein Kampf*.
5. **VIKING METAL** – White people? Check. Scandinavian? Check. Dig wacky helmets with horns? Check.
6. **TECHNICAL DEATH METAL** – If your fans can't really play your music in their bedrooms, shouldn't that be enough?
7. **MELODIC DEATH METAL** – Songs about raping rotting corpses . . . but with vocal harmonies and maybe some keyboards.
8. **GROOVE METAL** – I guess this means the band can play mid-tempo songs without fluctuating BPM?
9. **SHRED METAL** – This one is basically a big sandwich board proclaiming "Our band features a chronic masturbator who is obsessed with his hair and guitar magazines."
10. **STONER METAL** – Aren't most Metalheads high on something?

5 WORST ALL-TIME TRENDS IN METAL

by Bassist Extraordinaire Danny Lilker
(Nuclear Assault, S.O.D., Brutal Truth . . .)

They don't make 'em more real or true than Dan Lilker . . . or more talented, for that matter. He's the most genuine article around and has never given a fuck what you think. He's going to play what he's going to play, and thank god that's been his attitude. He's one of the only people who we approached about contributing to the book who we told, "Do whatever the hell you want," and we knew we'd wind up happy. Peep it:

NU METAL – Because it was nauseating watching a bunch of middle-class white dudes trying to be "street." Not to mention, the music had the dynamics of a light switch.

GRUNGE METAL – Goatees and plaid shirts . . . Whatever.

PORN GRIND – Offensive to half the human race.

FUNK METAL – Nothing wrong with RHCP, but when all these thrash bands all of a sudden were doing slap bass and stopped thrashing, I gotta say, it was a bummer.

HIPSTER BLACK METAL – OK, so your band plays minor chords over blast beats—but you're still wearing a knit hat.

SONGS: THE GOOD AND
THE TERRIFICALLY UGLY

OUR FAVORITE SONGS BY THE BEST METAL BANDS

Obviously this list is completely subjective. To include multiple great songs by each of these artists would simply take up too much space and mental energy. Therefore, we give you only one per band (or singer), and just know this: It's a GREAT one! After all, no matter the genre, the SONG is what makes you care about any band, and the manner in which it is performed seals the deal. What you'll find might not be each band's "signature" track, but it represents everything great about them and is uniquely identifiable as their respective brand of Metal.

1. BLACK SABBATH – OZZY "War Pigs" / DIO "Heaven and Hell"
2. IRON MAIDEN – DI'ANNO "Wrathchild" / DICKINSON "The Prisoner"
3. METALLICA – "Creeping Death"
4. SLAYER – "Raining Blood"
5. MOTÖRHEAD – "Iron Fist"
6. JUDAS PRIEST – "Breaking the Law"
7. EXODUS – "Bonded by Blood"
8. MANOWAR – "Manowar"
9. VENOM – "Black Metal"
10. ANTHRAX – "Soldiers of Metal"
11. SEPULTURA – "Inner Self"
12. MERCYFUL FATE – "A Dangerous Meeting"
13. CELTIC FROST – "Procreation (of the Wicked)"
14. VOIVOD – "Psychic Vacuum"
15. NUCLEAR ASSAULT – "Betrayal"
16. TESTAMENT – "Disciples of the Watch"
17. OBITUARY – "Chopped in Half"
18. FEAR FACTORY – "Replica"
19. MÖTLEY CRÜE – "Live Wire"
20. MEGADETH – "Wake Up Dead"

BEST METAL INSTRUMENTALS

Each component of a Metal band should ultimately serve to make the whole greater than any individual part. That said—if the MUSIC itself isn't killing, no vocalist in the world can polish an aural turd. Metal can be so intense sometimes that adding a singer into the mix can actually be doing a disservice to the piece of music. Here are ten examples of songs exclaiming, "We don't need no stinkin' lyrics!"

1. "THE CALL OF KTULU" – Metallica
2. "(ANESTHESIA) PULLING TEETH" – Metallica
3. "ORION" – Metallica
4. "20" – Karma to Burn
5. "GAME OVER" – Nuclear Assault
6. "TRANSYLVANIA" – Iron Maiden
7. "VOICE OF THE SOUL" – Death
8. "THE JESTER'S DANCE" – In Flames
9. "STING OF THE BUMBLEBEE" – Manowar
10. "FAR BEYOND THE SUN" – Yngwie J. Malmsteen

15 GREAT COVER SONGS BY METAL BANDS

Cover songs are always fun, even if they're awful, but they can also be a group's funeral. Release even a great one too soon in your career and it comes to define your band by default. Here are some that are damn good and do not take away from the original material these bands are known for:

1. METALLICA – "Last Caress/Green Hell" (Misfits)
2. IRON MAIDEN – "Cross-Eyed Mary" (Jethro Tull)
3. MOTÖRHEAD – "Louie Louie" (The Kingsmen)
4. SEPULTURA – "Policia" (Titãs)
5. SLAYER – "Guilty of Being White" (Minor Threat)
6. FEAR FACTORY – "Cars" (Gary Numan)
7. KILLSWITCH ENGAGE – "Holy Diver" (Dio)
8. TYPE O NEGATIVE – "Black Sabbath" (Black Sabbath)
9. KARMA TO BURN – "Twenty Four Hours" (Joy Division)
10. ANTHRAX – "Got the Time" (Joe Jackson)
11. BLIND GUARDIAN – "In A Gadda Da Vida" (Iron Butterfly)
12. CHILDREN OF BODOM – "Lookin' Out My Back Door" (Creedence Clearwater Revival)
13. MEGADETH – "These Boots Are Made for Walking" (Nancy Sinatra)
14. DESTRUCTION – "The Damned" (Plasmatics)
15. MUDVAYNE – "King of Pain" (The Police)

HEAVY METAL (VOCAL) COLLABOS

In the hip-hop universe, collaborations are a dime a dozen, but when it comes to Metal, they are few and far between, and good ones are even more difficult to find. Some of these are good, others, um . . . NO! However, an A for effort is in order here, as there are some legendary peeps involved. We're sure these all can be found on YouTube or elsewhere, so check 'em out for yourself.

1. OZZY OSBOURNE/LITA FORD – "Close My Eyes Forever"
2. LEMMY/WENDY O. WILLIAMS – "Stand By Your Man"
3. BRUCE DICKINSON/ROB HALFORD – "The One You Love to Hate"
4. DAVE MUSTAINE/CRISTINA SCABBIA – "A Tout le Monde (Set Me Free)"
5. PEPPER KEENAN/JAMES HETFIELD – "Man or Ash"
6. PHIL ANSELMO/TIM WILLIAMS – "By the River"
7. ILL BILL/MAX CAVALERA – "War Is My Destiny"
8. MAX CAVALERA/SEAN LENNON – "Son Song"
9. TOM ARAYA/ICE-T – "Disorder"

EACH AND EVERY HEAVY METAL REFERENCE MADE BY RAPPER ILL BILL IN HIS SONG "PEACE SELLS"

Most of you don't, but some of you may know that there are, in fact, a few rappers out there who are extremely well versed in, and passionate about, Metal. If you're familiar with Brooklyn's ILL BILL, his brother Necro, Philly's Vinnie Paz, or the handful of other Metal-loving emcee/producers, you are aware that these cats' Heavy Metal knowledge stretches far beyond Maiden and Priest or the Big 4. On Bill's second solo album, *The Hour of Reprisal*, a blatant nod to the greatest Thrash band on earth, he offered up the "Unauthorized Biography of Slayer," a start-to-finish account of the band's career from their first-ever tour to their current runnings. Hell, Bill and Vinnie even have a group together called Heavy Metal Kings. The music is dark as fuck and drenched with the exact same energy pulsing through the veins of even the most extreme Norwegian Black Metal group. Each of these guys can out-Metal even the most devoted Heavy Metal fan, and they are constantly out there letting their thousands of followers in on what's true and real. As an example, here is every single Metal reference (and a handful of hardcore ones too) made in ILL BILL's song "Peace Sells," which is featured on his 2004 album, *What's Wrong with Bill?*

PEACE SELLS

I'm the Kreator of Terrible Certainty, it's No Escape from the Toxic Trace
Pop your face, Storming With Menace and Blind Faith
The Angel of Death Read Between the Lies South Of Heaven
Expendable Youth, Divine Intervention
Teaching y'all a Lesson in Violence
Doctor Death injecting the virus, apocalypse
I'm a horseman in the Circle of Tyrants
and death's the era, Possessed like Jeff Becerra
Consuming Impulses drown you in the depths of terror, forever

(Chorus)
Peace Sells But Who's Buying?
Who's trying? who's crying? who's lying in a pool of blood dying?
Peace Sells But Who's Buying?
Who's trying? who's crying? who's poppin' with the four pound iron?
Peace Sells But Who's Buying?
Who's trying? who's crying? who's lying in a pool of blood dying?
Peace Sells But Who's Buying?
Who's trying? who's crying? who's lying in a pool of blood?

Stranded in Hell, My America dated Betrayal
Brainwashed by a system that's created to fail
Freedom or Fire, Securitron, ominous fate
Fear Factory manufacturing Hi-Tech Hate
A Slave New World, world gone mad, a World Without Heroes
Used to go to shows surrounded by weirdos
Live at L'Amours, mastering the science of war
Reading Metal Forces Magazines dying to tour
Biohazards and Carnivores, living a Life of Agony
Where to go, We Gotta Know like Harley Flanagan
Electric Funeral, Children of the Grave Behind the Wall of Sleep
Be afraid, killing to be saved
I Don't Need Society, Down for Life, foul and trife
Ill Bill, Dirty Rotten Imbecile, down to fight
Give Me My Taxes Back, money, God's a liar
Speak truth to Def Americans like Tom Araya

(Chorus)

Psychic Vacuum, jab you with a knife & stab you
Ravenous Medicine, Tribal Convictions, it's heroin
Experiment, Macrosolutions to Megaproblems
Let the revolvers solve 'em, Chaos Mongers, a Cosmic Drama
Peace Sells but Who's Buying, so I stay with the funds
We're real, so you die and find you laced with the slugs
With the Quickness you calling me my Sacred Love
I got Bad Brains, the reason I spray with guns, now listen

(Chorus)

THE 25 MOST FUCKED-UP SONG TITLES BY CANNIBAL CORPSE

Real talk: Cannibal Corpse is fucked-the-hell-up! If grindhouse movies had an unofficial soundtrack, it would certainly be any and all output from Chris Barnes and his not-so-merry band of psychopaths. Many a conservative politician has rallied against the band for "undermining the national character of the United States," among other things. Their music, as well as their album covers, has been banned in numerous countries, yet they soldier on to this very day, ruining people's meals everywhere they go. I salute you, Cannibal Corpse, for never caving in, and for providing the world with a consistent and thorough manner in which to make parents deathly afraid of their kids. These titles alone explain A LOT!

1. "Edible Autopsy"
2. "Bloody Chunks"
3. "A Skull Full of Maggots"
4. "Meat Hook Sodomy"
5. "Under the Rotted Flesh"
6. "Covered with Sores"
7. "Rancid Amputation"
8. "Innards Decay"
9. "I Cum Blood"
10. "Addicted to Vaginal Skin"
11. "Entrails Ripped from a Virgin's Cunt"
12. "Post Mortal Ejaculation"
13. "Fucked with a Knife"
14. "Stripped, Raped, and Strangled"
15. "Orgasm Through Torture"
16. "Dismembered and Molested"
17. "Raped by the Beast"
18. "Frantic Disembowelment"
19. "Blunt Force Castration"
20. "Rotted Body Landslide"
21. "Five Nails Through the Neck"
22. "Submerged in Boiling Flesh"
23. "Skewered from Ear to Eye"
24. "Followed Home Then Killed"
25. "Intestinal Crank"

RANDOM INFORMATION, THOUGHTS, AND SPECULATION

15 METAL ALBUM COVERS FEATURING GOATS

Because nothing says "Satan" quite like a goat!

1. BATHORY – S/T
2. BATHORY – Under the Sign of the Black Mark
3. DEATH ANGEL – Relentless Retribution
4. SLAYER – Show No Mercy
5. SLAYER – Reign in Blood
6. SLIPKNOT – Iowa
7. GOATWHORE - The Eclipse of Ages into Black
8. VENOM – Black Metal
9. VENOM – Welcome to Hell
10. WITCHFYNDE – Give 'Em Hell
11. MASTODON – The Hunter
12. NOCTURNAL GRAVES – Satan's Cross
13. BELPHEGOR – Bondage Goat Zombie
14. FUNERAL GOAT – Mass Ov Perversion
15. ABOMINANT – Triumph of the Kill

ALL HAIL THE ORIGINAL MAN—SOME METAL BANDS THAT HAVE, OR HAVE HAD, BLACK MEMBERS

It is a well-known fact that rock 'n' roll was stolen from the black man. And then whitey decided to take matters into his own hands and brought it on harder, faster, and with 33 percent more devil worship by inventing Heavy Metal. Here's to some proud Nubians who get down with the get-down:

1. KATON W. DE PENA – Hirax
2. LLOYD GRANT – Metallica
3. GREG FULTON – Znowhite/Cyclone Temple
4. HOWARD JONES – Killswitch Engage
5. DERRICK GREEN – Sepultura
6. LAJON WITHERSPOON – Sevendust
7. BYRON DAVIS – God Forbid
8. DUG PINNICK – King's X
9. ALL MEMBERS OF SOUND BARRIER
10. TERRANCE HOBBS AND MIKE SMITH – Suffocation
11. ALL MEMBERS OF BLACK DEATH

2 BAND NAMES SEPULTURA CONSIDERED USING BEFORE CHOOSING THE NAME SEPULTURA by Max Cavalera

1. TROPA DE SHOCK (in English: Shock Troops)
2. GUERILHA (in English: Guerilla)

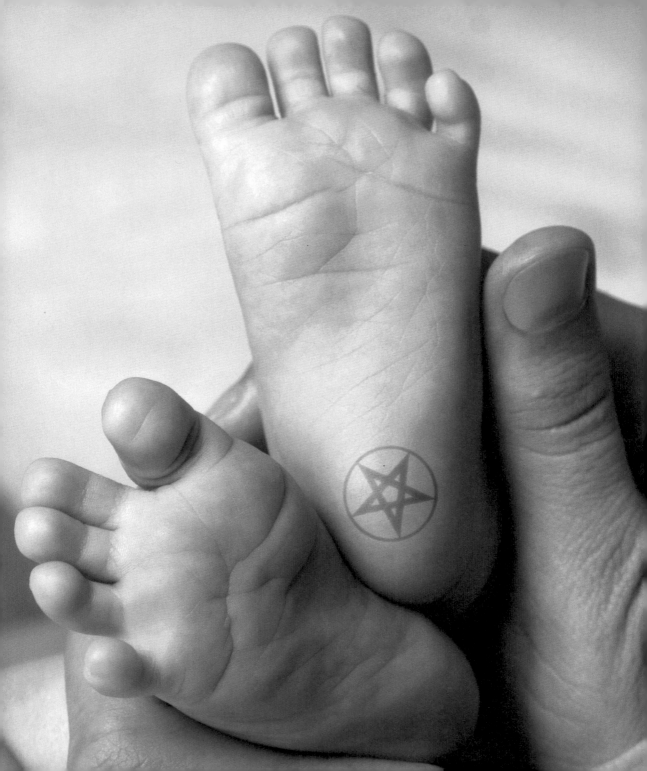

BIRTH NAMES OF METAL HEROES

Wouldn't it be great if you found out that your favorite Metal band member's real name was Lester or Irving or something old-person sounding? We think so too, so here you have some birth names of artists who use something other than what their parents gave them. Oh, and we're staying away from most Black Metal people, because that list would require its own book.

1. OZZY OSBOURNE – John Michael Osbourne
2. ROB HALFORD (JUDAS PRIEST) – Robert John Arthur Halford
3. BRUCE DICKINSON (IRON MAIDEN) – Paul Bruce Dickinson
4. SCOTT IAN (ANTHRAX) – Scott Ian Rosenfeld
5. TOM ARAYA (SLAYER) – Tomás Enrique Araya Diaz
6. DAVE MUSTAINE (MEGADETH) – David Scott Mustaine
7. TOM G. WARRIOR (CELTIC FROST) – Thomas Gabriel Fischer
8. ABBATH DOOM OCCULTA (IMMORTAL) – Olve Eikemo
9. GAAHL (GORGOROTH) – Kristian Eivind Espedal
10. SNAKE (VOIVOD) – Denis Bélanger
11. KING DIAMOND (MERCYFUL FATE/KING DIAMOND) – Kim Bendix Petersen
12. CRONOS (VENOM) – Anthony Bray
13. PETER STEELE (CARNIVORE/TYPE O NEGATIVE) – Peter Thomas Ratajczyk
14. ERIC ADAMS (MANOWAR) – Louis Marullo
15. CHUCK SCHULDINER (DEATH) – Charles Michael Schuldiner
16. VARG VIKERNES (BURZUM) – Kristian Larssøn Vikernes
17. QUORTHON (BATHORY) – Thomas Börje Forsberg
18. MICK MARS (MÖTLEY CRÜE) – Robert Alan Deal
19. LIPS (ANVIL) – Steve Kudlow
20. CHRIS BARNES (CANNIBAL CORPSE) – Chris Barnes

TOP 10 OBSCURE METAL BLADE RECORDS FACTS

by Metal Blade Records Big Kahuna Brian Slagel

1. The Goo Goo Dolls and Cannibal Corpse played shows together in Buffalo when both bands were starting out.
2. The original name of the label was going to be Skull and Crossbones Records, but that name was actually already taken.
3. It took six hours to record the drums for Slayer's *Show No Mercy*, and we had to overdub the cymbals due to the fact that they were "bleeding" into the mics.
4. The first record Brendan O'Brien ever produced was on Metal Blade. A band named Johnny's Law.
5. We did marketing for Faith No More's *The Real Thing*, Alice in Chains, Mother Love Bone, and more, back in the early '90s.
6. One of Zack Snyder's (*300*, *Watchmen*, etc.) first directing jobs was a Lizzy Borden video.
7. The only time Lars Ulrich has recorded with another band is on Mercyful Fate's *In the Shadows* album.
8. Mötley Crüe was supposed to be on the first Metal Massacre compilation but pulled out when their album *Too Fast for Love* started to take off.
9. Ron Fair, who discovered and produced Christina Aguilera, engineered Slayer's *Hell Awaits* album.
10. The mastering we did on the five Thin Lizzy albums we reissued has been used many times on subsequent reissues by other bands.

THE TOP 10 MOST-METAL HOCKEY PLAYERS, ACCORDING TO METAL BLADE RECORDS HONCHO BRIAN SLAGEL

1. **DREW STAFFORD (Buffalo Sabres)** – This guy knows his Metal big-time! He may know more underground Metal bands than I do. Great guy and player too.

2. **MIKE MCKENNA (St. Louis Blues)** – Another massive Metal fan. Everything from underground to the "right" big bands. He rules!

3. **TONI LYDMAN (Anaheim Ducks)** – Used to be Stafford's teammate in Buffalo. Big Metal fan. Goes to tons of shows in his native Finland in the off-season.

4. **JANNE NIINIMAA** – Played eight seasons in the NHL. He once spent a week on tour with Cannibal Corpse.

5. **JAROMIR JAGR (Philadelphia Flyers)** – I took him to meet Metallica when they were recording *Load*. Huge Metal fan, nice guy, and hockey legend!

6. **KEN BAUMGARTNER** – Played eleven seasons in the NHL, and also did a Metal single with us. It featured members of Armored Saint, Fates Warning, and Suicidal Tendencies.

7. **TUUKKA RASK (Boston Bruins)** – The new number-one goalie is also a big Metalhead!

8. **CRAIG LUDWIG** – Played for the Dallas Stars and is a good friend of Vinnie Paul's. He knows his Metal.

9. **JERE LEHTINEN** – Another former Dallas Stars player who is a big Metal fan. What's going on in Dallas?

10. **ANDREW PENNER** – Just-retired, former minor league star is a massive Metal fan. Another player who knows his stuff!

MEGAFORCE RECORDS FUN FACTS
by Jon and Marsha Zazula

1. What Megaforce lead singer became the frontman for Accept? Mark Tornillo of TT Quick
2. What Mega guitarist went on to become the lead guitarist for the Grateful Dead? Warren Haynes
3. What Mega band was almost burned to death while shooting their album cover? Overkill
4. What historic album was recorded during the downtime of Anthrax's *Spreading the Disease* sessions? S.O.D.'s *Speak English or Die*
5. When Ace Frehley met with the Zazulas at a super-posh restaurant in New York City, he surprised everybody by ordering what modest entrée? A tuna fish sandwich
6. What lead guitarist in the Mega family was also in Trans-Siberian Orchestra? Alex Skolnick of Testament
7. Who was the infamous Lone Rager, and what Adrenalin PR person appeared on the chorus? Megaforce boss Jon Zazula and daughter Rikki Zazula
8. Where were the post-Metallica Megaforce releases recorded? Pyramid Studios, Ithaca, New York
9. Who produced Anthrax's first single? Manowar's Ross the Boss
10. Which Mega drummer wore a hockey helmet to protect himself when head-bashing cymbals? Raven's Rob "Wacko" Hunter

10 INTERESTING MOMENTS FROM THE KILL 'EM ALL FOR ONE (METALLICA/RAVEN) U.S. TOUR

by Raven's John Gallagher

As a teenager, the excitement surrounding the Kill 'Em All for One tour was equivalent to a modern-day teen's joy over the announcement that Justin Bieber and Rihanna are heading out on the road together . . . except we all know that such a pairing would represent the coming of the apocalypse. Metallica was touring in support of the (then) blueprint for thrash, *Kill 'Em All*, and UK heroes Raven were bringing it to the States—we believe for the first time—to showcase the excellent *All for One*. A truly groundbreaking moment in Metal's history. John was kind enough to share with us a few fun behind-the-scenes glimpses into the tour.

1. "IF WE DON'T GET A HOTEL ROOM, WE ARE GOING BACK HOME, NOW!!!"
   (Me, to tour manager Tony on day 3, with no sleep!)

2. Cliff Burton quote: "DONT FUCK AROUND!!!"

3. Another Cliff Burton quote: "OH FUCK, OH FUCK!!!" (as Mark and Rob start
   fighting in the dressing room, while standing on Cliff's backup bass).

4. The line that preempted us traveling in the back of the truck for most of the
   tour: "Whaddya mean you can't shit in the Winnebago toilet???"

5. "AAAAAAAAGGGGGGHHHHHHH!" (My quote, after turning on the light inside
   the back of the truck and being faced with maybe fifty mosquitoes.)

6. Bald Knob, Arkansas. Seriously . . . BALD KNOB?!

7. "Tony, can I have the keys to the white truck?" (Lars, grinning, with dubious
   female in tow, wanting "private time.")

8. The smell of that Winnebago after the toilet door was ripped off its hinges
   by Cliff Burton . . .

9. As the Winnebago threw a rod and died, the sight of Lars running away from
   the burning wreck at Olympic speed!

10. Roadie to Metallica member: "I MIGHT HAVE TO WORK FOR YOU, BUT I DON'T
    HAVE TO EAT NEXT TO YOU—FUCK OFF!"

Honorable mention: At a Mexican restaurant, Mark and Cliff, crying with laughter
and pointing at a half-eaten burrito: "IT'S ILLNESS ON A BUN!" Ahhhhh . . .
good times!!!

TOP 10 EARLY RAVEN RECORDING FACTS

by Raven's John Gallagher

1. The intro to "Rock Until You Drop" consists of us stamping on plastic coffee cups in a stone bathroom.

2. There is an Italian pressing of *Rock Until You Drop* that has no sound effects on the song "Tyrant of the Airways"! [May be my favorite Raven song. —Howie] Neat Records was so cheap, they gave the Italian licensee a rough mix.

3. The end of the song "Wiped Out" features a garbage can filled with metal objects being thrown down the studio's stone stairs. If you crank it loud enough, you can hear our roadie John Lowdon shouting, "What the fuck was that?!"

4. The guitar Mark used on *Wiped Out* cost about twenty bucks from a thrift store.

5. All the songs for *Wiped Out* and the *Crash Bang Wallop* EP were recorded and mixed in one week.

6. The only effects unit at Neat Records' studio was a Roland Space Echo . . . Echo . . . Echo . . .

7. During the solo on "Hold Back the Fire," Mark was jumping up and down on top of the studio piano—the solo was played live with the band.

8. At the end of "Chainsaw," Rob plays "Chopsticks" and I play "Side by Side" on the piano at the same time.

9. The talking between the tracks on *Rock Until You Drop* was so amusing to the album's producer, Steve Thompson, that he begged us to leave it on, starting a tradition of sorts, as we usually tape all the nonsense that goes on. Pure comedy!

10. The *Rock Until You Drop* album cover was set up at our rehearsal room, and the guy who was sent to do the shots was a wedding photographer—the look on his face was priceless!

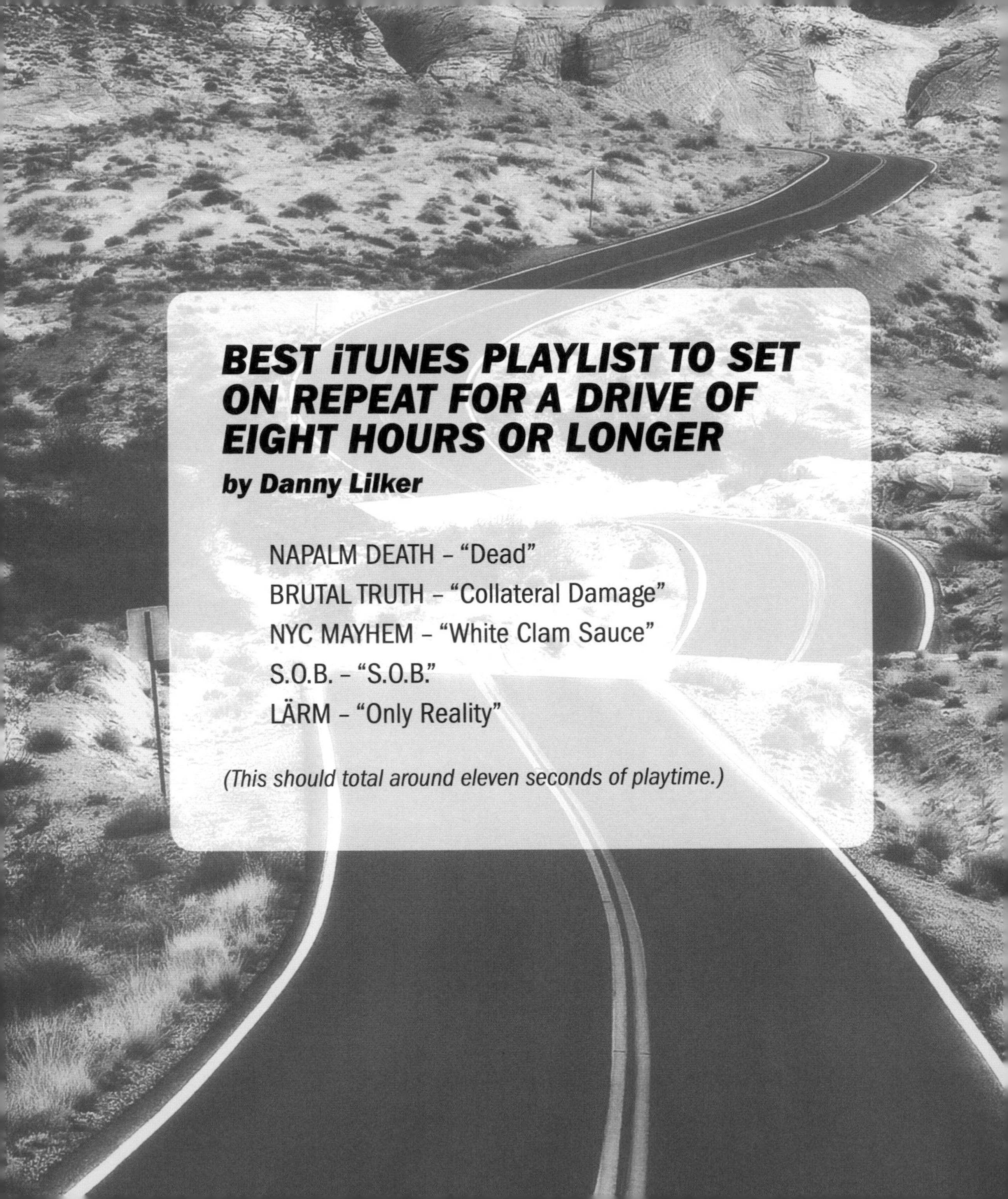

BEST iTUNES PLAYLIST TO SET ON REPEAT FOR A DRIVE OF EIGHT HOURS OR LONGER

by Danny Lilker

NAPALM DEATH – "Dead"

BRUTAL TRUTH – "Collateral Damage"

NYC MAYHEM – "White Clam Sauce"

S.O.B. – "S.O.B."

LÄRM – "Only Reality"

(This should total around eleven seconds of playtime.)

WHERE ARE THEY NOW?
THE MTV HEADBANGER'S BALL *EDITION*

Love(d) it or hate(d) it, *Headbanger's Ball* has had a tremendous impact on the world of heavy music since its launch in 1987. It allowed Heavy Metal to thrive in the video age, which MTV basically created, and was absolutely instrumental in bringing a number of bands to the attention of those living above and beyond the underground. While Metal was still uniformly ignored by radio stations and mainstream media, the *Ball* actually took a handful of chances over time and supported some HEAVY bands. While it was still airing on MTV proper, none of its hosts really represented Heavy Metal as a whole very well, and as was the case with a couple of them, not at all. So for the few of you who give a rat's ass, here's what they're up to now:

1. **KEVIN SEAL** – He did a bit of acting (was unemployed?) after departing the *Ball*, and also did some voice-over work for the Cartoon Network. These days, Kevin's been trying to convince people that he works atop Seattle's Space Needle and manually operates its aircraft warning light, turning it on and off in one-second intervals. Uh . . . who cares?

2. **ADAM CURRY** – Not long after splitting with the channel, the man who may be the most recognizable MTV VJ of all time, and a podcasting legend, launched what would prove to be a very successful web portal and design firm (through which he actually owned the domain mtv.com, for which he would later be sued). His company eventually employed hundreds of people and was bought out by a giant corporation for mad loot. Today, Adam is a government legislation analyst, whatever the fuck that is.

3. **RIKI RACHTMAN** – Post HBB, Riki, who really only got the MTV gig because he was pals with Guns N' Roses and Mötley Crüe, held an interviewer's gig with World Championship Wrestling, and also had a radio slot in conjunction with NASCAR. He later hosted the painfully awful *Rock of Love* and banged some porn stars, including Janine, who not so quietly has made the Sunset Strip rounds a few times over. Yuck!

4. **DOMINICK DeLUCA** ("Man on the Street") – Dom owns a great skate/sneaker/apparel shop in L.A., called Brooklyn Projects in honor of his BK roots. He has initiated some pretty awesome collaborations with a number of kick-ass bands.

5. **JAMEY JASTA** – Hatebreed main man Jamey Jasta is still doing what he was doing prior to anchoring the HBB lead spot: recording and touring with Hatebreed, recording other projects, and making guest-vocal appearances all over the place.

BANDS, BANDS, AND MORE BANDS

THE 10 BEST HEAVY METAL BANDS TO FORM SINCE THE TURN OF THE (NEW) MILLENNIUM

Let's face it, we're not the youngest fellas in the world, so it's a bit more difficult to stay on top of what the younger generation brings forth the way we used to. With that, some damn decent Metal bands have been born in the last decade and a half or so. Sadly, we can't honestly say most of these rank up there with the all-time faves, but several of these bands received a lot of play during the writing of this here book. Check them out, and keep that fire burning.

1. GOJIRA *(They were Godzilla until 2001 or so . . .)*
2. MASTODON
3. GHOST
4. NAILS *(We don't give a fuck about classifying them . . . BRUTAL!)*
5. DRAGONFORCE *(They didn't use the name until 2002. Call it cheating, if you like . . .)*
6. AGALLOCH
7. KYLESA
8. NACHTMYSTIUM
9. AS I LAY DYING
10. WINTERSUN

THE 10 GREATEST DEATH METAL BANDS EVER

According to Monte Conner

We're not the biggest Death Metal fans, probably for the same reason we're not much into horror movies—and that's because we find them silly. After a certain age (fifteen?), the subject matter just isn't shocking, evil, or even funny anymore. However, some of the music these bands produced is gloriously brutal. Monte is an old friend who knows DM like the back of his bald little head, so we thought it would be best to leave this one to the expert. For the record, we do not consider number 5 to be "Death Metal," but fuck it, another Celtic Frost mention works for us.

1. DEATH
2. DEICIDE
3. MORBID ANGEL
4. OBITUARY
5. CELTIC FROST
6. CANNIBAL CORPSE
7. SUFFOCATION
8. CARCASS
9. ENTOMBED
10. POSSESSED

10 METAL BANDS WITH "DEATH" IN THEIR NAMES

Because Death is the only sure thing in life . . .

1. DEATH
2. DEATH ANGEL
3. MEGADETH
4. MERCILESS DEATH
5. NAPALM DEATH
6. DEATHRASH
7. DEATHSPELL OMEGA
8. NECRODEATH
9. HOBBS ANGEL OF DEATH
10. BLACK DEATH

10 BEST METAL BANDS FROM OUTSIDE THE UNITED STATES

by Max Cavalera

1. GOJIRA
2. KRISIUN
3. KORSUS
4. QUESTIONS
5. KREATOR
6. DESTRUCTION
7. ENTOMBED
8. CONTRIVE
9. TRIPTYKON
10. WORMROT

5 BANDS THAT COULD HAVE TURNED THE "BIG 4" INTO THE BIG 5

The "Big 4" of Thrash Metal is an accurate grouping. Each band helped popularize Thrash and brought it to the masses, although only one, the mighty Slayer, could still really be considered "Thrash" after they broke, so to speak. This punk-and-hardcore-drenched movement was the best thing to happen to true Metal since the New Wave of British Heavy Metal gave us Maiden and Priest. Beyond said "Big 4" is a handful of bands that, at one point or another, shed a great deal of influence onto Metal as a whole, and were only steps away from expanding the Big 4 into a possible Big 5, 6, 7, 8, or 9. Here are some thoughts on what may have kept that from occurring.

EXODUS

Honestly, Exodus is probably the one band that truly deserved to be the heir to the Big 4's fifth throne. Their lineage is deeply rooted in the same places as Metallica, and of course, they gave Kirk Hammett over to Met (whether they wanted to or not). Hell, guitarist Gary Holt even filled in for Slayer's Jeff Hanneman at the NYC Big 4 gig, as well as at others. Their debut album, *Bonded by Blood*, is one of the finest slabs of Heavy Metal ever released, and the riffs are absolutely bombastic! Then there's Paul Baloff . . . an absolute legend. What made him incredible is also what probably kept the band from becoming bigger than they did. His screech can make your skin crawl at times, but Paul's overall delivery made one want to kill posers, which, of course, was his sole purpose in life. Sure, they eventually brought Zetro into the fold on vocals, but Baloff helped create Exodus' identity, and once that was gone, so was the band's true essence. Regardless, Exodus is an incredible band, and we all miss Paul. However, Paul being Paul is why they must remain on the fringe.

Suggested listening – *Bonded by Blood*

TESTAMENT

Testament has been a band stuck "in between" on a number of levels. Born out of the Bay Area's Legacy, these guys could riff with the best of them, and Alex Skolnick is one of the finest guitar players in all of Metal. Chuck Billy is (literally) a tremendous frontman and a decent vocalist, but his range always proved to be limited, leaving the group unable to stretch themselves beyond their exceptional musicianship. Generally, their combination of Exodus-style riffing and Billy's only-serviceable vocals keeps Testament out of the Big 5 running and relegated to the title of "Good Band."

Suggested listening – *The Legacy* and *The New Order*

NUCLEAR ASSAULT

While certainly musically competent and powerful, NA's strength exists in their ability to successfully combine Thrash with a genuine punk/hardcore sensibility rarely evidenced in the Metal world. Lyrically, they tackled subjects ranging from war and strained interpersonal relationships to the environment and even animal rights. Bassist Danny Lilker is an absolute beast on the four-string, and he taught Anthrax a thing or two while a member of that band—things for which he never receives the proper credit. John Connelly's voice brought the tension and chaos necessary to top off Nuclear Assault's sound, but unfortunately, it annoyed the shit out of a lot of people, similar to the way Paul Baloff's did. Even though John helped complete the group's identity, he may have kept them from rising to higher ground. Still, an all-time fave of ours.

Suggested listening – *Survive* and *Handle with Care*

SEPULTURA

Far and away the greatest Thrashers to ever emerge from outside the United States. The Cavalera brothers, Max and Igor, forced their way through the Metal door with their unique brand of speed, precision, and Third World angst. When these guys released *Beneath the Remains* in 1989, you knew it was ON, and this Brazilian quartet had truly arrived. While the diehards started to bitch and whine about the band, from the release of the *Arise* album and on, Sepultura continued to put on one of the most intense live shows of any band and toured the world with absolutely everyone. Difficult to blame the wall they eventually hit on this, but the language barrier and Max's heavy accent didn't help matters for Sep in live situations. Even though "FUCK SHIT UP" became a rallying cry for their fans, the Portuguese language may ultimately be what kept Sepultura from completing the Big 5. A devastating band, nonetheless.

Suggested listening –
Beneath the Remains, Arise, and *Chaos A.D.*

OVERKILL

Things were off and running for Overkill very early on, as *Power in Black* was one of the most important Metal demos during the heyday of tape trading. Gaining a following all over the place, due to the tape's wide distribution and their energetic live shows, it would have been easy to think that these guys were going to take the slot Anthrax eventually occupied in the Big 4. Then again, Overkill's recorded output was "uneven," to say the least, and their latter-day performances bordered on total cheese. They remained a force for quite a while, but just never seemed to evolve musically or lyrically enough to capture the hearts or imagination of the grander Metal universe.

Suggested listening – *Power in Black* demo

BAND NAME ACRONYMS

Bands, fans, and journalists are equal parts lazy, crazy, and bored to death. Remember all the people who tried to read into what "KISS" stands for? Apparently, it simply stands for "money," as far as Gene $immon$ is concerned, but thanks to our less-motivated traits as human beings, we've actually shortened the names of hundreds of bands over the years. Yes, the guys in S.O.D. wanted to be known as S.O.D., probably because of D.R.I. and C.O.C., but originally they named themselves Stormtroopers of Death. We guess if you want an encore after the set is over, an acronym makes for easier chanting.

1. W.A.S.P. = We Are Sex Perverts
2. STRYPER = Salvation Through Redemption, Yielding Peace, Encouragement, and Righteousness
3. R.A.V.A.G.E. = Raging Atheists Vowing A Gory End
4. DBC = Dead Brain Cells
5. ENT = Extreme Noise Terror
6. I.N.C. = Indestructible Noise Command
7. D.R.I. = Dirty Rotten Imbeciles
8. C.O.C. = Corrosion of Conformity
9. R.D.P. = Ratos de Porão
10. CKY = Camp Kill Yourself

SOME NON-METAL ARTISTS METALHEADS LOVE

Let's face it, anything can eventually become boring, even if the feeling is only temporary, so when punters began to tire of Metal a bit in the late '80s/early '90s, they stumbled upon a new crop of bands combining all kinds of styles with a similar intensity and even heaviness to what they'd always known and loved. Here are thirty-five examples:

1. PRIMUS
2. FAITH NO MORE
3. N.W.A.
4. SOUNDGARDEN
5. BEASTIE BOYS
6. NIRVANA
7. PUBLIC ENEMY
8. RAGE AGAINST THE MACHINE
9. SUICIDAL TENDENCIES/ INFECTIOUS GROOVES
10. BAD BRAINS
11. MISFITS
12. CHARGED G.B.H.
13. DISCHARGE
14. 24-7 SPYZ
15. EINSTÜRZENDE NEUBAUTEN
16. ALICE IN CHAINS
17. AGNOSTIC FRONT
18. CRO-MAGS
19. SKINNY PUPPY
20. ROLLINS BAND
21. MR. BUNGLE
22. NIN
23. MINISTRY
24. PEARL JAM
25. HELMET
26. MELVINS
27. GODFLESH
28. WHITE ZOMBIE
29. CYPRESS HILL
30. VAN HALEN
31. D.R.I.
32. (EARLY) CORROSION OF CONFORMITY
33. DEAD KENNEDYS
34. SEX PISTOLS
35. JANE'S ADDICTION

BEST SUGGESTED PACKAGE TO TOUR THE DEEP SOUTH

by Danny Lilker

IMPALED NAZARENE
GOATWHORE
BLASPHEMY
NUNSLAUGHTER
IMPIETY

*Of course, if Anal Cunt was still around, they'd headline.

EDDIE TRUNK'S "TOP 5 BANDS YOU PROBABLY NEVER HEARD OF THAT I THINK SHOULD HAVE BEEN HUGE"

Eddie Trunk is one of the good guys. When no one was carrying the flag forward on behalf of Heavy Metal and hard rock, Eddie took that shit and ran fast and far. If you listen to him on the radio and/or watch *That Metal Show*, you are aware that he brings the Metal, as well as the hard rock, like nobody's business. While not necessarily Metal, the bands that Mr. Trunk lists here are ones he believes deserved more attention from Heads' ears than they received.

1. **D GENERATION** - NYC band that came on the scene in the early '90s at the height of the grunge movement and represented the complete opposite. Raw hard rock band with a punk edge, great songs, great live show. I thought they were the next Guns N' Roses. After three major label releases, the band broke up, but they reunited in 2012 and plan to make a new album, so maybe there is hope after all?

2. **ICON** - Arizona band. First came on the scene in the early '80s with a crushing self-titled debut on Capitol. They followed it with a total direction change into a more melodic hard rock sound, which also worked brilliantly and earned them huge critical praise (especially in the UK) for their second album, *Night of the Crime*. I then signed the band to Megaforce in 1987, and they released *Right Between the Eyes*, with a slightly different lineup. Great production and songs—loved them. They try to do stuff from time to time, but they're not all that active anymore.

3. **TT QUICK** - Debut full-length, *Metal of Honor,* is essential heavy rock for fans of AC/DC, Accept, etc. Early '80s New Jersey legends who guitarist Dave DiPietro hugely influenced and who taught a young Jersey kid named Jeff Weilandt, aka Zakk Wylde. Singer Mark Tornillo joined Accept in 2010, and to date has recorded two great comeback albums with the German legends.

4. **VAIN** - Bay Area band from the mid-'80s. Singer Davy Vain had star quality, and even though the band had a glam look, they had a raw dual guitar in-your-face attack. Debut album, *No Respect*, is a total classic.

5. **UFO** - They're in this spot only because they did have much more success than the above bands, but they're still, to this day, MASSIVELY underrated here in the United States. My all-time favorite band that I am always turning people on to, and they thank me for it. UFO's influence is all over the place; Iron Maiden open every show playing "Doctor Doctor" over the PA system. More than forty years on, they are still touring and making great new music. Greatest melodic hard rock band ever!

SLICING JA...
BROUGHT UP TO WASTE MANKIND
LOKI'S PETS HIS LITTLE CHILDREN
DEADLY EVERY TIME

TRAPPED IN SWAMPS BY GATES OF HELL

DON'T EVER LET THEM OUT
FOR IF YOU DO AND THE...
YOU'LL F... ... A...Y BOUT

PIRANHA KILL IN A PACK - YOU'LL ...
PIRANHA START TO ATTACK - YOU'LL DONE
IF YOU THINK YOU CAN BEAT - DEADLY SCHOOL
IF YOU THINK YOU CAN LIVE - YOU'RE A FOOL

GATES OF HELL ARE OLD AND CRACKED
THEY TUMBLE AND THEY FALL
OUT RUSH A BLOODY WALL OF DEATH
TO KILL ... AT ...
THEIR SOLE MISSION IS TO KILL
STRIP YOUR BONES AND FLESH
RIP OUT YOUR EYES TEAR OFF YOUR FACE
AN AGONIZING DEATH

10 SONGS TURNED BAND NAMES

Most bands claim that the single most difficult thing to do is agree on a name for their band. We call that BULLSHIT! Just read the lyric sheet inside your favorite album and try to say there aren't at least a handful of ideas to choose from. Here are ten band names, as well as the bands whose songs influenced their moniker.

1. MOTÖRHEAD – Hawkwind
2. OVERKILL – Motörhead
3. SAINT VITUS – Black Sabbath
4. GODSMACK – Alice in Chains
5. FIREHOUSE – KISS
6. PIRANHA – Exodus
7. BONDED BY BLOOD – Exodus
8. MR. BIG – Free
9. MACHINE HEAD – Deep Purple
10. JUDAS PRIEST – Bob Dylan

PIRANHA KILL IN A PACK - YOU'LL RUN
PIRANHA START TO ATTACK - YOU'RE DONE
IF YOU THINK YOU CAN BEAT - DEADLY SCHOOL
IF YOU THINK YOU CAN LIVE - YOU'RE A FOOL

Because you'll get more gigs with the name KISS than you will with FUCK.
That's right—KISS actually considered calling themselves "FUCK"!

1. Earth to Black Sabbath
2. Brats to Mercyful Fate
3. Mantas to Death
4. Xecutioner to Obituary
5. Kaos to Hirax
6. Band X to Accept
7. Meld to Slipknot
8. R.A.V.A.G.E. to Atheist
9. Legacy to Testament
10. Forbidden Evil to Forbidden
11. Repulsion to Sub-Zero to Type O Negative
12. Nihilist to Entombed
13. Ulceration to Fear Factory
14. Knight of Demon to Destruction
15. Tormentor to Kreator

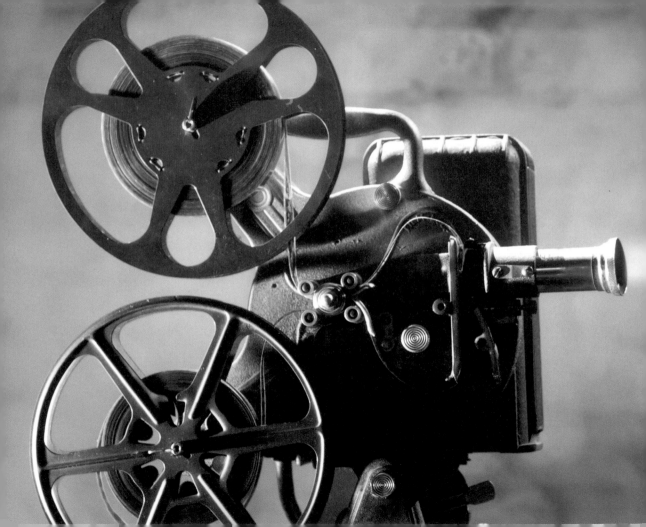

METALLULOID

THOROUGHLY EMBARRASSING METAL VIDEOS

Honestly, this is a stupid list to put in a book, because you can't immediately link to any of these cinematic tragedies, but what the hell. Go to YouTube, or wherever else, and behold. You'll be begging us to get your [insert length of video here] back! So bad . . . but so worth at least one viewing, for a chuckle.

1. ALTERNATE REALITY – "The King That Never Was"
   We still can't tell if they're a terrible Metal band with the world's most awful video, or an incredible Oi! band with an awful video. Either way, this is terrible.

2. GRIM REAPER – "See You in Hell"
   We're pretty certain the only reason anyone has ever heard of Grim Reaper is because of this video . . . and that's a BAD reason!

3. JUDAS PRIEST – "Hot Rockin'"
   It all makes sense now. Rob Halford fantasized about making this clip since the early days of JP. A dream cum true, really.

4. IMMORTAL – "Call of the Wintermoon"
   We love Immortal, and Black Metal for that matter, as much as the next Satan-loving sadist, but if we want to see people running around in the woods acting douchey, we'll watch *The Blair Witch Project*.

5. CANDLEMASS – "Bewitched"
   We have to wonder what the band members thought when they saw this footage for the first time. "Does this Friar Tuck thing make my ass look fat?"

6. THOR – "Anger Is My Middle Name"
   What ISN'T embarrassing about this video??? We liked it better when he was blowing up hot water bottles in the hope they would pop.

7. HALFORD – "Made of Metal"
   You know: The video of the giant gorilla/dinosaur/ninja turtle flying the spaceship/car, cut with the cheesy, video game–looking race cars . . . Nuff said.

8. ARMORED SAINT – "CAN U DELIVER"
   People waited a pretty long time for a video from these guys, and the first 1:22 of this medieval retard fest is mortifying. Not even the pack of Headbangers, who appeared in the video for free beer, can save this hunk of crapola.

9. TWISTED SISTER – "Heavy Metal Christmas"
   This is so much worse now than when it first infected our souls. One of the reasons that bands like Twisted Sister wore all of the crap that they did was because each and every member is fucking UGLY. The best gift from Santa would be to never have to see any of these dudes sans makeup and costume ever again.

10. U.D.O. – "I Give as Good as I Get"
    This is like watching your decrepit, Depends-wearing grandfather die before your very eyes. A slow, painful demise.

Rock Star, with Mark Wahlberg and Jennifer Aniston? Nah! These are real-deal, Oscar-worthy pieces of celluloid made in the true spirit of Metal. If you haven't seen all five, put down the PBR and finish your hot wings. Each deserves your eyes and ears (assuming you still have them).

1. HEAVY METAL PARKING LOT

This bit of docu-genius, created byJeff Krulik and John Heyn in 1986 at Landover, Maryland's Capital Centre, could not possibly have been scripted better. They interviewed fans outside the arena at a Judas Priest concert, doing what tailgating fans do hours before their heroes take to the big stage: drinking, drinking, and more drinking, which results in some of the greatest hesher commentary EVER captured. This is a MUST see.

2. THIS IS SPIÑAL TAP

Almost any band member will tell you how closely this mockumentary represents the lives and activities surrounding a touring Metal band. We're not sure we can pinpoint which band(s) this is most accurately in tune with, but it doesn't really matter. *Tap* shines in its utter insanity and ridiculous glory. A true classic.

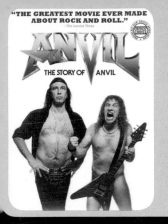

3. ANVIL: THE STORY OF ANVIL

I cannot recount how many times I saw Anvil play back in the early '80s, although it was more than I can count on two hands. While I never envisioned Anvil ever becoming a "big" band, Lips's attire and antics are legendary, and the Metal community embraced the band as if they were heroes. If you've seen the film, you know the story, and it's as triumphant as it is tragic. I'm just happy that these guys got their shining moment with it.

4. LAST DAYS HERE

A can't-look-away gander into (a bit of) the life story and current circumstances of Pentagram's Bobby Liebling. As a band, Pentagram isn't all that far off from Sabbath, but truth be told, Bobby's behavior makes Ozzy Osbourne look like Gandhi. With Liebling holed up in his parents' basement chasing imaginary parasites and smoking crack, superfan and manager Sean Pelletier's quest to resurrect Bobby's career seems impossible. But you have to admire Sean's determination, and anyone willing to stretch themselves this far for their favorite Metal band deserves a medal. The film is so creepy at times, you will cringe in your seat.

5. METALLICA: SOME KIND OF MONSTER

We all know Metallica likes to take chances—some terrifically off the mark, such as the Lulu "experiment," and others brilliant, such as this film. While a lot of "real" 'tallica fans inexplicably hated this, we were captivated by its warts and all-out honesty. Then there's Dave Mustaine coming face-to-face with his former bandmates . . . Maybe that's why some fans wish this movie had never seen the light of day. Dave whining and crying about getting thrown out of the biggest, most successful Metal band of all time isn't a good look—unless you're Metallica, hoping to make a compelling documentary. The therapy sessions are a bit awkward too, but that's what therapy is, and I praise Metallica for letting us in on it.

IT'S NOT EASY BEING . . .

10 THINGS YOU SHOULD KNOW ABOUT BEING BLACK IN A METAL BAND

Hirax's Frontman Katon W. De Pena

1. Times have changed . . . It's not like it was in the early 1980s, when I first started. It's a lot easier to be a person of color singing in a Heavy Metal band now.
2. No matter how good you are, somebody will still be against you just because of your color. There are a lot of people that are still racist, but you can't let it bother you.
3. You have to work harder than ever before, because the heroes that came before you (e.g., Jimi Hendrix, Phil Lynott) are legends, and you owe it to them—to pay them respect by being great at what you do.
4. It's okay to let people know that you don't like rap music!
5. If you're going to play Heavy Metal music, you have to play it from the heart. NO POSERS!!!
6. You must be willing to sacrifice a normal life.
7. You must be open-minded about all forms of Heavy Metal music—no matter what!
8. You'll have to get used to not sleeping very much and also traveling on long plane/ bus/car rides.
9. Never let your fans down!
10. There is no such thing as "making it overnight"!

*There are more black-skinned Metal fans than you will ever know!

THE BEST AND WORST THINGS ABOUT BEING IN A METAL BAND FROM BRAZIL

by Max Cavalera (Sepultura, Soulfly, Cavalera Conspiracy)

Not many people can be considered true Metal warriors, but Max Cavalera takes the cake. Born and raised in the southeast Brazilian city of Belo Horizonte, he and his brother Igor not only sought out the most underground Metal around at the time, but also took it, improved upon it, and ran with it BIG-time! Sepultura is an amazing and classic band with an equally amazing history of hard work, drive, and perseverance. Sep's music has always been as angry as Max, and we doubt very highly that even he ever imagined the possibilty of combining the spirit of Metal with that of Brazil and bringing it to millions of Headbangers worldwide. Max was kind enough to offer up a little insight into what it has been like to be in one of the all-time greatest Metal bands and hail from Brazil. "Fuck Shit Up!"

WORST THINGS

1. Money – We were flat broke, so we had to steal our first equipment (like microphones, etc.).
2. Location – We're far away from the rest of the world. Not too many bands came to Brazil in the beginning.
3. No support from radio, TV, or promoters. Heavy Metal was an underground movement in Brazil.

BEST THINGS

1. Culture – Brazil's culture is very rich and powerful. The *Roots* album is a perfect example: Anger from being from a Third World country without money, and dealing with lots of prejudice from society in general.
2. The colors – We introduced the yellow and green into the Metal scene.
3. Being from a different country made us exotic and exciting.
4. I eat great! My wife is a super cook. She even learned how to make my favorite Brazilian meal, feijoada. I get to see her all the time on tour, and have family on tour as well. It's great! She lets me sleep late, and we never have to worry about anything. Everything's taken care of, from passports to hotel rooms to sound checks to interviews. Everything runs smoothly because Gloria's in charge.

TOP 11 THINGS PEOPLE SAY TO START A CONVERSATION WITH ME

by Anthrax's Scott Ian

As far as recognizable band members go, Scott Ian is a pretty approachable fella. However, Metalheads are an awkward breed, so try to picture some of the less socially . . . um, "savvy" fans trying to engage him in a conversation. None of these surprise us in the least:

1. "Aren't you the singer of Anthrax?"
2. "Aren't you the bass player of Anthrax?"
3. "Aren't you that guy from System of a Down, Pantera, Live?"
4. "I recognize you—are you on TV?"
5. "Do you still play music?"
6. "I used to listen to you."
7. "What band are you in?" "Anthrax." "No, that's not it." (An actual conversation)
8. "Hey, you're Flea from the Red Hot Chili Peppers!" "No, I'm not." "Don't be a dick about it, dude. I KNOW you are him." (Another actual awesome conversation)
9. Preface anything with "I don't mean to bother you, but . . . "
10. "Scream my name at me REALLY loud."
11. "Can I touch your beard?"

WE ARE THE ROAD CREW!

Some notable band members whose humble beginnings included lugging gear, tuning guitars or drums, copping drugs, and, naturally, securing groupies for the fellas:

1. Lemmy was a roadie for Jimi Hendrix before joining Hawkwind and later forming Motörhead.
2. Dark Angel's Gene Hoglan was an early drum tech for Slayer's Dave Lombardo.
3. Every member of Coroner was a Celtic Frost roadie before forming their own band.
4. Death Angel's Mark Osegueda is a former Exodus roadie.
5. Frank Bello was a roadie and guitar tech for Anthrax before replacing Dan Lilker on bass.
6. Billy Howerdel worked as guitar tech and Pro Tools engineer for Tool before he started A Perfect Circle with Maynard James Keenan.
7. John Marshall was a Metallica roadie before joining Metal Church.
8. Doug Piercy of Heathen/Anvil Chorus/Control was a roadie for Exodus.
9. Joey DeMaio of Manowar was a pyrotechnician for Black Sabbath on their Heaven and Hell tour.

THE 10 BEST AND WORST THINGS ABOUT BEING A FEMALE FRONTING A METAL BAND

by Bitch's Betsy Weiss

For those who don't know, Betsy was a MAJOR underground Metal sex symbol when Bitch's first EP and album came out on Metal Blade Records in 1982. In fact, Bitch was the FIRST-EVER band signed to Metal Blade, and they appeared on the very same *Metal Massacre* compilation that featured Metallica's first commercial release, "Hit the Lights." Bitch's shows were legendary, and Betsy did an awful lot for Metal over the years, so we want to make sure she has a say in these here pages.

BEST:

1. Being showered with attention.
2. Being an accepted member of the "All Dudes Club" that's synonymous with the genre of music.
3. Feeling like "one of the guys" (please also see number 2).
4. Getting to wear tight black leather pants, studded armbands, and a rhinestone bra onstage.
5. Being the focal point of the band.
6. Not having to carry equipment.
7. Male groupies.
8. Fronting an awesome Heavy Metal band, and getting to rock out and look good doing it.
9. Playing the character of "Betsy Bitch."
10. Having the opportunity to get out there on that stage and do it just as well as (if not better than) the guys.

WORST:

1. Not being taken seriously as a musician.
2. Having people be shocked that I can actually sing well.
3. Not being able to turn my vocal cords up to "10" like the guys get to do with their Marshall amplifiers.
4. Having to respond to interview questions such as "Are you really into bondage and discipline and S&M in real life?"
5. Having to share a dressing room with horny male musicians.
6. Taking two hours before a gig to do my hair and makeup to perfection, only to sweat it off under the stage lights and end the set looking like a drowned rat.
7. Having to work out for ninety minutes every other day to continue looking good in those tight leather pants and rhinestone bras I previously mentioned.
8. Not being able to wear the same jeans and tank top I showed up to sound check in for the actual show like the guys do.
9. Having to constantly see my first name in print with the letters *t* and *s* transposed. (Please see: "Besty" Bitch.)
10. Not making the decision to have breast implants about twenty years ago—might have given my career a kick in the chest . . . so to speak.

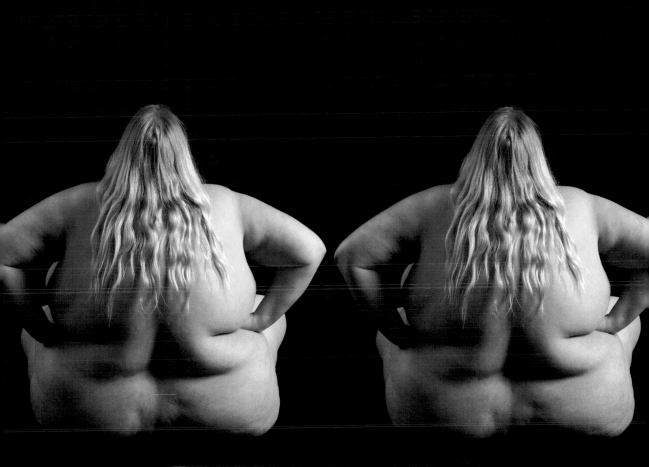

THE BIG 4:
METAL RECORD LABEL EDITION

ROADRUNNER RECORDS

COMBAT

METALBLADE RECORDS

MEGAFORCE RECORDS ™

THE BIG 4:
METAL RECORD LABEL EDITION

Before there ever could have been a Big 4 of bands, there was a Big 4 of Heavy Metal record labels. At one point, whatever any of these labels was set to release was already well in demand by the die-hard underground fans, who would run to stores by the thousands to snap up these classic releases. Each label was run by passionate people who gave a shit about the music and wanted to bring the best bands to the forefront. Don't get it twisted . . . Record labels were, and always will be, a business, so money was huge in the overall equation, but there were definitely easier ways to make money than financing underground Metal. Nuff respect to all who passed through these seminal labels, past and present—bands and employees. For all intents and purposes, they are the reason a book like this could even exist. Here are a few of the absolute gems to come from the Big 4 of Metal labels.

MEGAFORCE RECORDS

1. METALLICA – Kill 'Em All
2. METALLICA – Ride the Lightning
3. ANTHRAX – Fistful of Metal
4. S.O.D. – Speak English or Die
5. TIED: OVERKILL – Feel the Fire / MANOWAR – Into Glory Ride

METAL BLADE RECORDS

1. SLAYER – Show No Mercy
2. VOIVOD – War and Pain
3. FLOTSAM AND JETSAM – Doomsday for the Deceiver
4. HIRAX – Raging Violence
5. SACRED REICH – Ignorance

ROADRUNNER RECORDS

1. MERCYFUL FATE – Melissa (Europe Only)
2. ANNIHILATOR – Alice in Hell
3. SEPULTURA – Beneath the Remains
4. OBITUARY – Slowly We Rot
5. CARNIVORE – S/T

COMBAT RECORDS

1. MEGADETH – Killing Is My Business . . . and Business Is Good
2. EXODUS – Bonded by Blood (in conjunction with Torrid Records)
3. NUCLEAR ASSAULT – Game Over
4. POSSESSED – Seven Churches
5. DARK ANGEL – Darkness Descends

METAL ON METAL

70 METAL SONGS ABOUT METAL

"Bang your head as if up from the dead, intense metal is all that you need"
—Exodus, "Bonded by Blood"

1. "METAL ON METAL" – Anvil
2. "WHIPLASH" – Metallica
3. "METAL MILITIA" – Metallica
4. "BONDED BY BLOOD" – Exodus
5. "METAL COMMAND" – Exodus
6. "THE TOXIC WALTZ" – Exodus
7. "THRASH UNDER PRESSURE" – Exodus
8. "BLACK METAL" – Venom
9. "TOO LOUD (FOR THE CROWD)" – Venom
10. "METAL PUNK" – Venom
11. "HARDER THAN EVER" – Venom
12. "METAL BLACK" – Venom
13. "MIND OVER METAL" – Raven
14. "THRASH ATTACK" – Destruction
15. "FIST BANGING MANIA" – S.O.D.
16. "MILANO MOSH" – S.O.D.
17. "UNITED FORCES" – S.O.D.
18. "CELTIC FROSTED FLAKES" – S.O.D.
19. "SHRED" – Overkill
20. "IN UNION WE STAND" – Overkill
21. "SOLDIERS OF METAL" – Anthrax
22. "METAL THRASHING MAD" – Anthrax
23. "HEAVY METAL CHRISTMAS" – Twisted Sister
24. "I WANNA ROCK" – Twisted Sister
25. "HEAVY METAL HUNTER" – Metalucifer

26. "HEAVY METAL CHAINSAW" – Metalucifer
27. "RATTLEHEAD" – Megadeth
28. "METAL HEART" – Accept
29. "SLAVES TO METAL" – Accept
30. "SHAKE YOUR HEADS" – Accept
31. "HAMMERHEAD" – Overkill
32. "HEAVY METAL MANIAC" – Exciter
33. "HEAVY METAL (IS THE LAW)" – Helloween
34. "HEAVY METAL UNIVERSE" – Gamma Ray
35. "LET THEM EAT METAL" – The Rods
36. "POWER THRASHING DEATH" – Whiplash
37. "METAL QUEEN" – Lee Aaron
38. "HIGH SPEED METAL" – Razor
39. "BULLET BELT" – Gama Bomb
40. "METAL HEALTH" – Quiet Riot
41. "HEAVY METAL" – Thunder
42. "LISTEN TO HEAVY METAL THUNDER" – Thunder
43. "THE METAL" – Tenacious D
44. "DIO" – Tenacious D
45. "HEAVY METAL IS FOREVER" – Metal Law
46. "THE BOOK OF HEAVY METAL" – Dream Evil
47. "HEAVY METAL FIRE" – Stormwarrior
48. "DENIM & LEATHER" – Saxon
49. "HEAVY METAL THUNDER" – Saxon
50. "DENIM AND LEATHER" – Saxon
51. "METALHEAD" – Saxon
52. "METAL WILL NEVER DIE" – Dio
53. "DEATH TO ALL BUT METAL" – Steel Panther
54. "METAL SHOP" – Metal Shop
55. "HEAVY METAL" – Judas Priest
56. "HEAVY METAL NEVER DIES" – Iron Savior
57. "METAL GODS" – Judas Priest
58. "HOT ROCKIN'" – Judas Priest
59. "ROCK HARD RIDE FREE" – Judas Priest
60. "ROCK YOU ALL AROUND THE WORLD" – Judas Priest
61. "MONSTERS OF ROCK" – Judas Priest
62. "METAL MELTDOWN" – Judas Priest
63. "METAL MESSIAH" – Judas Priest
64. "METAL MAGIC" – Pantera
65. "HEAVY METAL RULES" – Pantera
66. "ONWARD WE ROCK" – Pantera
67. "POWER METAL" – Pantera
68. "PROUD TO BE LOUD" – Pantera
69. "THE ART OF SHREDDING" – Pantera
70. "THE UNDERGROUND IN AMERICA" – Pantera

A DOZEN MANOWAR SONGS ABOUT METAL

"'Cause only one thing really sets me free / Heavy metal, loud as it can be!"
—Manowar, "Metal Daze"

1. "METAL DAZE"
2. "DEATH TONE"
3. "GLOVES OF METAL"
4. "BLACK ARROWS"
5. "THUNDERPICK"
6. "BLOW YOUR SPEAKERS"
7. "DRUMS OF DOOM"
8. "KINGS OF METAL"
9. "METAL WARRIORS"
10. "BROTHERS OF METAL PT. 1"
11. "THE GODS MADE HEAVY METAL"
12. "MANOWARRIORS"

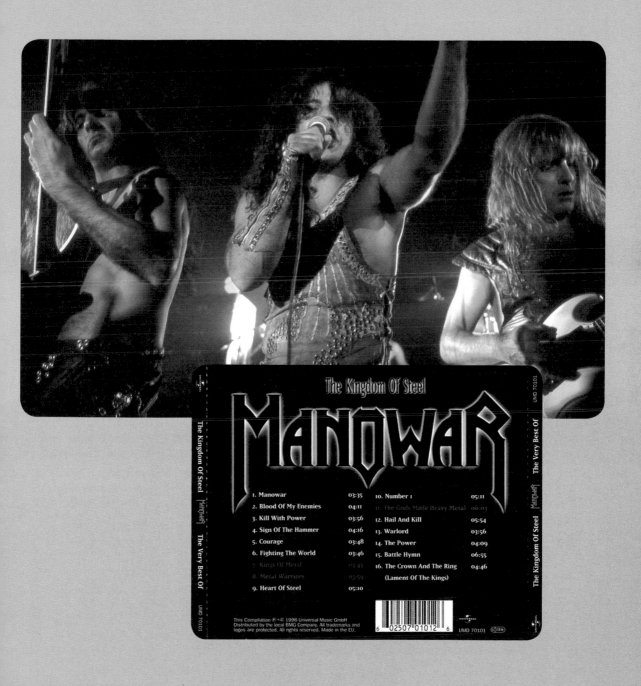

The Kingdom Of Steel

MANOWAR

The Very Best Of

1. Manowar   03:35
2. Blood Of My Enemies   04:11
3. Kill With Power   03:56
4. Sign Of The Hammer   04:16
5. Courage   03:48
6. Fighting The World   03:46
7. Kings Of Metal   03:43
8. Metal Warriors   03:59
9. Heart Of Steel   05:10

10. Number 1   05:11
11. The Gods Made Heavy Metal   06:03
12. Hail And Kill   05:54
13. Warlord   03:56
14. The Power   04:09
15. Battle Hymn   06:55
16. The Crown And The Ring   04:46
    (Lament Of The Kings)

This Compilation ℗ + © 1998 Universal Music GmbH
Distributed by the local BMG Company. All trademarks and
logos are protected. All rights reserved. Made in the EU.

UMD 70101

6 02507 01012 6

AND YOUR MOTHER DRESSES YOU FUNNY

10 HEAVY METAL FASHION FAUX PAS

Metal has always had a distinct look, but never any actual fashion sense whatsoever. The denim and leather uniform came about so that we could identify each other, but truth be told, it's a pretty shitty look. For some it may qualify for the "guys want to be like them" portion of the rock star rules, but it definitely does not satisfy the "girls want to sleep with them" part, unless of course you dig low-self-esteem chicks who hate authority and are overflowing with Daddy issues. Here are ten no-no's if you play in a Metal band and want someone—anyone—to respect what you have to offer:

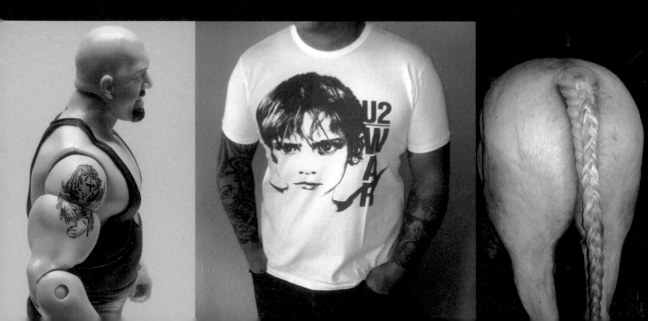

1. More than one member wearing the band's T-shirt onstage or for a photo shoot. C'mon, do your friggin' laundry, or at least talk to each other before the show.
2. Wearing a bullet belt with shorts. We love the bullet belt, but with shorts it just screams "Heavy Metal homelessness."
3. Putting your hair in a ponytail. You've obsessed over your locks since you were a teenager for precisely these very moments when you could let it flow in front of a crowd. Are you THAT lazy?
4. Stretchy bike shorts. Unacceptable. You're not Lance Armstrong, and unless you are hung like a donkey, it's just a bad move.
5. Emulating the style of your favorite member of a bigger band who is still alive. Overkill's Bobby Gustafson comes to mind when he mysteriously morphed into . . . *And Justice for All*–era James Hetfield. Creepy and stalkerish.
6. "Borrowing" a trendy fashion item from a lesser-known band and acting as if it's your own. Board shorts, Suicidal Tendencies–style trucker hats with the brim turned upward, braces (skinhead-style suspenders) . . . If it's not really you, leave that shit alone.
7. Rocking a T-shirt with the sleeves cut off, revealing your one, embarrassingly small, poorly executed tattoo. Come to think of it, tattoos are so mainstream now, having only one shitty piece that says "Fuck the World (F.T.W.)" might make you look legit. Okay—no it doesn't.
8. Wearing sweatpants on stage or for a photo shoot. My friends, the "no image" approach IS, in itself, an image. Sweatpants are symbolic of not giving a crap about yourself, the fans . . . or anyone. We'd rather see you back in the spandex you were rocking during your Quiet Riot phase.
9. Wearing the shirt of an extreme Metal band when your group sounds like a bunch of pussies. If you sound like Europe or Autograph, not even wearing a Mayhem shirt can give you cred.
10. The unironic sporting of a Bjork, U2, or Coldplay shirt. If you do this, you obviously HATE Metal and are disguising it by trying to show people how "diverse" your tastes are. Fuck you!

Honorable mention: Alice Cooper, looking like evil Alice one day and sporting Callaway golf gear on the links the next, makes us cringe.

A HIPSTER'S GUIDE TO METAL T-SHIRTS

Metal T-shirts are probably second only to skinny jeans in the hipster fashion arsenal. They sport them, more often than not, with irony as a societal fuck-you, but while they're busy listening to Liturgy, the real Metal kids are thinking of ways in which to end these hipsters' lives without getting caught. Here is the Hipster Metal T-shirt Hall of Shame:

1. **BURZUM** – Even though none of these dicks are aware that they are repping an arson-happy neo-Nazi, Burzum tees can be found scattered throughout Passion Pit shows nationwide.

2. **IRON MAIDEN** – We're convinced that not a one could name a single Maiden song, let alone one with AND without Paul Di'Anno.

3. **METALLICA** – Probably the only jerks who like *Load* and/or *Reload*, thanks to Lollapalooza. However, they rock *Master of Puppets* instead, because the skaters told them to.

4. **ANTHRAX** – For no other reason than the band did a joint with Public Enemy . . . who the hipsters don't know shit about either.

5. **SLAYER** – Because the dude who cleared off their table at the gourmet taco spot was wearing one, and he was infinitely cooler than them.

6. **MOTÖRHEAD** – A few nights later, they saw the guy who cleared off their table at the gourmet taco spot out at a bar, and he was wearing one, so they had to have one too. Never even heard "Ace of Spades."

7. **SLAYER** – Had to list it twice, 'cause you see SO MANY of them!

8. **MÖTLEY CRÜE** – They think it'll get them chicks.

9. **MUNICIPAL WASTE** – They're convinced it's a "classic" Thrash band, so now they think they are up-to-speed with the cool kids.

10. **VENOM** – The shirt says "Black Metal" on it, so naturally they have to get down with the "next big thing."

THE WHITE MAN CAME ACROSS THE SEA

TOP 10 NWOBHM BANDS YOU DON'T KNOW
by Metal Blade Records Big Cheese Brian Slagel

1. **MYTHRA** – Truly amazing band that put out only one EP. "Death and Destiny" was one of the best NWOBHM songs.

2. **URCHIN** – Adrian Smith from Iron Maiden's original band. Just put out a few 7-inches, but really good stuff.

3. **QUARTZ** – You may actually know them, as they put out quite a few albums but still go unnoticed. "Satan's Serenade" is one of the best songs from the NWOBHM.

4. **WHITE SPIRIT** – Janick Gers's original band. Very heavy Deep Purple influence.

5. **TRESPASS** – Another one that, if you'd really paid attention, you might know. Killer stuff here.

6. **WEAPON** – One of the more influential bands from the NWOBHM that never really went too far. "Set the Stage Alight" was a hit at the time.

7. **OVERDRIVE** – Some really classic NWOBHM here. Sadly, they did not do much.

8. **BLACK AXE** – Another killer band that put out only a couple of 7-inches. Pretty heavy stuff.

9. **HOLLOW GROUND** – A true classic, and the hard-core fans of the movement know them well.

10. **A II Z** – They're almost one you might know . . . but still obscure. The song "Treason" is amazing.

10 HORRIFICALLY BAD NWOBHM BANDS

As far as the family tree of Metal goes, you could argue that no modern HM band would even exist without all that the NWOBHM brought to the game. When we were *Kerrang!*-obsessed youngsters, we would read about these bands in every single issue . . . and then we would listen to them. Several were so great and game changing, and we awaited their arrival on this side of the pond for what seemed like an eternity. But the others: Holy crap were we disappointed! We'd convinced ourselves that we'd be hearing a hundred new Iron Maidens . . . but not so much. It doesn't mean a hill of beans how influential some of these bands were on Metallica, or which bands Chris Tsangarides produced. While clearly an extremely important movement in the big scheme of Metal, these, and most other NWOBHM bands, get the gas face!

1. TYGERS OF PAN TANG
2. DEMON
3. BATTLEAXE
4. DUMPY'S RUSTY NUTS
5. ROCK GODDESS
6. THUNDERSTICK
7. VARDIS
8. PRAYING MANTIS
9. MAMA'S BOYS
10. GASKIN

THE 10 BEST NWOBHM BANDS

On the other hand, these bands are fucking great!

1. IRON MAIDEN
2. JUDAS PRIEST
3. MOTÖRHEAD (SORT OF NWOBHM)
4. VENOM (DITTO TO MOTÖRHEAD)
5. SAXON
6. DIAMOND HEAD
7. RAVEN
8. DEF LEPPARD (EARLY DAYS)
9. TANK
10. ANGEL WITCH

10 UK THRASH BANDS THE REST OF THE WORLD (THANKFULLY) IGNORED

No one can deny the influence of the NWOBHM, but when it comes to Thrash, the UK was straight-up soft, yo! Seriously, we don't think we've ever heard a pure Thrash band from England that moved us in the least bit. Here are ten subpar groups from the bottom of Britain's barrel:

1. ONSLAUGHT
2. ATOMKRAFT
3. ACID REIGN
4. XENTRIX
5. RE-ANIMATOR
6. TORANGA
7. SABBAT
8. DEATHWISH
9. SLAMMER
10. SACRILEGE

10 REASONS DAVE MUSTAINE PROBABLY DECLINED TO PARTICIPATE IN THIS BOOK

It's really not worth getting into all of the reasons why many folks cannot stand Dave Mustaine. His antics are legendary and have proven to be self-destructive on an unfathomable level. By all accounts, he's got A LOT of issues, and while drugs and alcohol have been among them, those indulgences are only a fraction of the problem. He believes himself to be larger than life, which many rock stars do, but he's that guy who would probably snap his fingers at a waiter if he felt his salad was taking too long to be delivered to the table. Ultimately, Dave owes a lot of people an awful lot for assisting him with his recovery, as well as his career. Sadly, we don't think he sees it that way, and he was THE ONLY person to out-and-out decline to be involved in this book, with absolutely no explanation. Dave doesn't owe us anything, really, but it just provides us with another reason to keep him off the list of those who give back to the community that spawned and supported him. Since Dave wouldn't get down with us, we can only assume what it was that was more important for him to spend his time on.

1. He knew that any list about him would be a "worsts" list.
2. He was practicing his guitar-solo snarl in front of his bedroom mirror with a tennis racket for the umpteenth time.
3. He was contemplating excuse number 4,687 for why he was kicked out of Metallica—for something that wasn't his fault.
4. He's still coming to grips with all of the youthful Satan-loving he engaged in as a kid now that he's a born-again.
5. It's hard to lie about yourself in someone else's book.
6. Mr. Mustaine was dreaming up new ways to blame President Obama for shit he couldn't possibly be responsible for.
7. He wouldn't be able to throw anyone out of Megadeth while he was busy writing a silly list.
8. Dave was wrapped up in meetings with Garnier Fructis, negotiating to be the face of their new hair-care products.
9. He was hard at work on the follow-up to his first book, tentatively titled *How to Lie About Absolutely Everything in Your First Book, but Still Have It Sold as a "Memoir."*
10. He was still searching for the letter *a* that fell out of "Megadeth."

10 REASONS THERE IS NO NEED TO HAVE A LIST CONCERNING OZZY OSBOURNE IN THIS BOOK

1. His "little friend" behind the amps at his gigs wasn't available to put words in his mouth.
2. Shaaaaarrrrrooooon most definitely wouldn't approve of its inclusion without a fee.
3. His dealer wasn't able to come through with an eightball of ants to snort, so he's unavailable to participate anyway.
4. Sharon was too busy firing Bill Ward to help out with much of anything else.
5. Only his daughter Aimee agreed to an interview, and frankly, who gives a shit?!
6. The Prince of Darkness allowing his manager/wife to be a judge on a show like *America's Got Talent* is about as un-Metal as it gets.
7. Ozzy, I mean, Sharon is STILL in the studio with Rob Trujillo and Mike Bordin, overseeing the sessions as they replace all of the parts that were played by Bob Daisley and Lee Kerslake on Ozzy's albums.
8. Bruce Dickinson isn't around to fight back.
9. Jack isn't well, and we don't want to rag on his parents TOO much.
10. *The Osbournes* says it all, anyway.

10 REASONS ANTHRAX SHOULD NEVER BE ASSOCIATED WITH HARDCORE
by Madball's Hoya Roc

Anthrax caused a big ol' stink in the mid-'80s by allegedly attempting to trademark the NYHC symbol, one that is exclusively associated with New York City's vibrant hardcore scene. Longtime scenesters were horrified and angered by it and let it be known that they weren't about to let this gesture go unnoticed. Chalk it up to Anthrax's misguided attempt to show some love, or a desperate credibility grab, but this was a bad look for 'thrax, and some have not forgiven them to this day. NYHC hooligan and Madball bassist Hoya Roc is one of them, so . . .

1. Going to a (hardcore) show once every leap year doesn't make you part of a scene.
2. Going bald and then fronting like you shaved your head on purpose doesn't make you hardcore.
3. Synchronized stage moshing is corny!
4. The "NOT MAN"??? WEAK!!!
5. Destroying Public Enemy's "Fight the Power."
6. Never taking a hardcore band on tour!
7. Dissed hardcore until they figured out they would never be Metallica.
8., 9., AND 10. Attempting to trademark the NYHC symbol makes them officially the WACKest wannabe, never-was band to try and claim the glory of hardcore music!!!

10 OBSERVATIONS FROM LEMMY'S WARTS

Lemmy is a god! His inimitable bass tone and vocal style are legendary, and so are his facial warts. Actually, those bad boys are so big, both literally and figuratively, that they must be recognized for what they truly are: carbuncles. Man, the things they've seen . . . Since Lemmy's carbuncles were unavailable for comment, we're going to assume that these are some of the gems they would have let us in on.

1. "When Lemmy's drugs wore off, he realized that Hawkwind SUCKED!"

2. "Partying with the members of Girlschool was fun; seeing them naked, not so much."

3. "Sometimes we have to remind Lemmy what the lyrics are to 'Ace of Spades.'"

4. "We're not big fans of his World War II relics collection. We have Jewish carbuncle friends and find it distasteful."

5. "We've begged Lem for years to switch to downers (the other stuff keeps us up all night)."

6. "Wendy O. Williams, God rest her soul, was a goooood time!"

7. "When Lemmy decided to move to Los Angeles from the UK, we bitched and moaned because we had to give up our Stoke City season tickets."

8. "Usually Lemmy isn't actually that fond of the road crew."

9. "We have no fucking idea what 'Killed by Death' means either."

10. "We wish Lemmy would go to another bar once in a while. We're so over the Rainbow."

WWVD:
WHAT WOULD VARG (VIKERNES) DO?

Is there any more notorious a figure on the Metal scene than Varg Vikernes, aka Count Grishnackh, aka Burzum? No, there is not. He's a murderer, an arsonist, and—oh yeah—he makes the worst Heavy Metal music EVER! I mean, seriously—Burzum sucks, and anyone who wears a Burzum T-shirt is only doing so for shock value. We thought it would be interesting, to say the least, to explore just what Mr. Grishnackh might do in some common situations. Read on, friends, read on . . .

1. *If he needed to resort to torture to teach someone a lesson, what would Varg do?*
   If one had to guess, he would subject them to one of the shite, faux-classical opuses he recorded while in the clink. Wagner he is not (although they're both total Nazis)!

2. *If he had a cell mate who played Lil Wayne all day, what would Varg do?*
   Obviously, this couldn't happen (have you ever seen a black man in Norway, except for when Hirax or Sepultura is on tour?), but I suppose he would show his celly what "chopped and screwed" REALLY means.

3. *If he were to be accused of murder, as well as arson, for burning down at least four churches, what would Varg do?*
   We know what Varg would do. He would spend only three-quarters of his twenty-one-year sentence behind bars, where he would record several new albums, become a full-blown National Socialist, and eventually be released to live on as if none of this had ever happened.

4. *If Gaahl from ex-Gorgoroth asked him out to dinner and a movie, what would Varg do?*
   First and foremost, Varg would let Gaahl know that he will not pick him up at that godforsaken shack he lives in in the middle of nowhere, and he would also make it clear that he doesn't kill or torture on the first date.

5. *If he read this list, what would Varg do?*
   Varg will never read this list for the simple fact that it has been compiled by a Jew and a black man!

10 THINGS METALHEADS SHOULD AVOID SAYING WHILE ONLINE DATING

The human dating ritual is extremely awkward, and so are Metalheads for the most part. Put them together and the result will likely be a laugh-out-loud train wreck for the ages. For whatever reason, most people are still completely baffled by online dating, even though it is probably more prevalent than meeting someone face-to-face these days. Personally, we believe the Internet is perfect for Heavy Metal mating. You can behave however you want, with no fear of having your boys overhearing you getting all mushy and admitting you kinda like Adele. None of the items below should leave your outbox if you want to close the deal:

1. "The spandex you're wearing in your profile photo makes your ass look like Hetfield's in '84."
2. "My uncle got me into Metal. We listened to a lot of Sabbath while showering together."
3. "Wanna meet at my trailer and smoke some ANGEL DUST???"
4. "I'm sooooo FUCKED UP right now!"
5. "Most chicks tell me I look like a cross between Brad Pitt and Lemmy."
6. "SLAYERRRRRRRRRRRRRRRRRRRRRRRR!!!" (Actually, if this one gets you laid, marry the girl.)
7. "I can totally relate to Dave Mustaine—my dreams are often crushed because of my alcoholism too."
8. "Burzum? Yeah, but I only like the Casio keyboard Nazi stuff that Varg produced in jail."
9. "Yeah, I have three older brothers. It's tough being the Anthrax of the family."
10. "I KNOW my profile says I'm 'in a relationship.' Utah's just different than other places."

Motörhead main man, and epitome of health and wellness, Lemmy Kilmeister, will make your skin shine and your soul smile with this intensive care program.

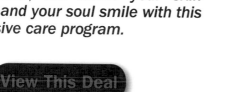

View This Deal

10 HEAVY METAL LIVINGSOCIAL/GROUPON DEALS YOU WILL NEVER SEE

Who doesn't love a great deal, but it's safe to say no one will ever be offered these "bargains":

1. 75% off facial from Lemmy
2. Buy one, get one free Bikram yoga class with Gene Hoglan from Dark Angel
3. 50% off Christian Bible study retreat with Gaahl from Gorgoroth
4. One complimentary vegetarian-cooking class with Chris Barnes from Cannibal Corpse
5. Discounted English diction class with Away from Voivod
6. Five free beauty tips from Sacred Reich's Phil Rind
7. Embracing Serene Passivity course, taught by Max Cavalera—first three classes free
8. $100 off one-week juicing cleanse with Fear Factory's Dino Cazares
9. Half-off trip for two to the United States Holocaust Memorial Museum in Washington, D.C., with Varg Vikernes

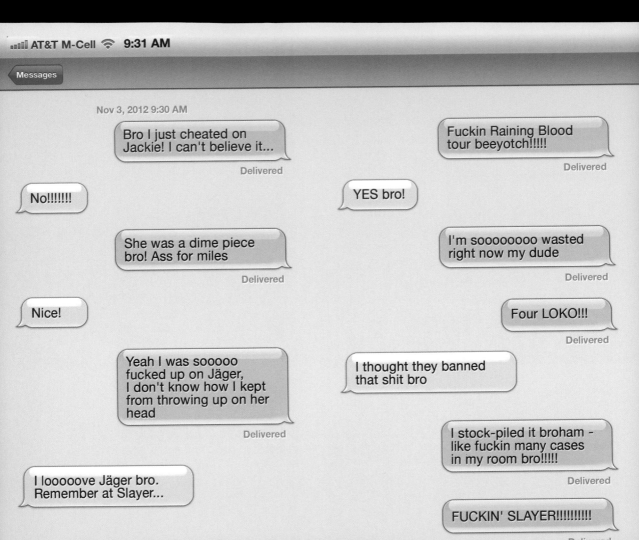

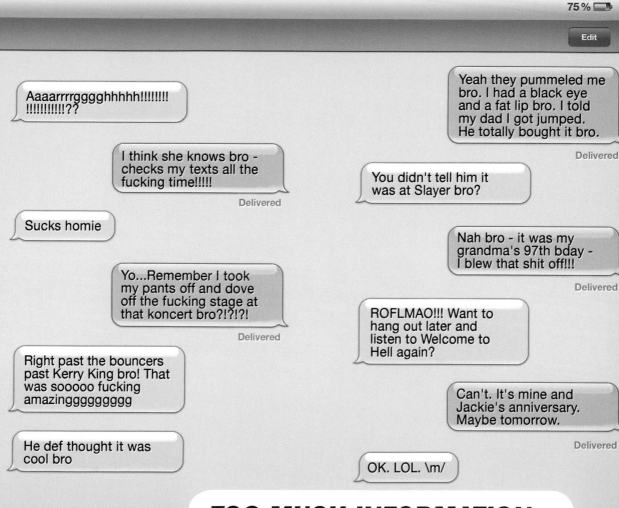

TOO MUCH INFORMATION

THE 5 CRAZIEST THINGS RICHARD CHRISTY HAS DONE ON TOUR IN HIS LIFE

by Richard Christy

CHARRED WALLS OF THE DAMNED / *THE HOWARD STERN SHOW*

Richard is fucking nuts! Most people know him from his gig on *The Howard Stern Show*, but the Metal community is familiar with him because he's an amazing drummer and has held it down for groups such as Death, Iced Earth, and his most recent outfit, Charred Walls of the Damned. If you're a *Howard* listener, you know that all of this "shit" is pretty normal for Mr. Christy. If you've just eaten, you might want to skip this one and read it in a few hours.

1. Crapped in a coffee can and then cooked it in the oven for an hour at 400°F. It happened during a gig at a community center in Missouri with my band Public Assassin, in the early '90s. It was something to do while waiting to go onstage. The building filled with the worst-smelling smoke ever while we were playing!

2. The Quadruple Poople. At a gig in northern Kansas, in the middle of nowhere, with my old band Public Assassin, after all of us had eaten Taco Tico Sanchos and had full bowels, the members of the band and our friends all decided to crap in one toilet without flushing. Needless to say, by the time my friend Brandon, who was last in line, took his turn, the feces were well above the top of the bowl. Disgusting.

3. Puked all over my feet while listening to Manowar on the tour bus in Austria. In 1998, when I was on tour with Death, we had a day off after our gig in Vienna, Austria, and I downed about three bottles of Applecorn, a delicious German apple wine, and puked all over my Converse All Stars while listening to the album *Kings of Metal* by Manowar. It was my most Metal puking ever! Our soundman was an angel and got me and the tour bus lounge cleaned up; I'll forever be in debt to him for that.

4. Pissed my pants on purpose while watching Iron Maiden in Milan, Italy. It was at the 2000 Gods of Metal festival, and I was touring with Demons and Wizards. We were opening for Iron Maiden, and after our set I started downing beers and went out to the soundboard scaffolding to watch one of my all-time favorite bands, MAIDEN!!! I had the best seat in the house, right above the soundboard. Unfortunately, when I had to pee about four songs in, I didn't want to wade a half mile through the crowd to go backstage to the restroom, so I did what any Maiden-loving Metalhead who doesn't want to miss any Maiden songs while pissing would do: I pissed in my pants. I ended up pissing myself about two or three times during the show and didn't miss any songs! I think I can safely say that I'm a true Maiden fan!

5. Got dressed in nothing but suspenders, Groucho Marx glasses, and a leopard skin T-back to sing with the band the Waffleheads onstage in Atlanta. It was the last night of the 1998 Death/HammerFall tour, and we wanted to do something special to end the tour. We all LOVED Waffle House, and we loved this band called the Perpetrators, who had a song out called "Let Your Tongue Roll Over My Bunghole," so we decided to play that song and call ourselves the Waffleheads, with everyone from the tour—bands and crew—onstage for the show-ending song. I was the singer, and I looked like an idiot. The audience didn't know what to think. They stared at us with their jaws wide open. It was the perfect reaction and an awesome way to end the funnest tour that I've ever been on!

READING IS FUN-DA-METAL

5 THINGS I LEARNED BY OPENING SLAYER'S FAN MAIL BACK IN THE DAY

by MC Serch (3rd Bass)

Although I am not what most would consider a Metalhead by any stretch, I do have an acute connection to Slayer. When we were tied together through Rush Management and Def Jam Records back in the '80s, to kill time I would open Slayer's fan mail and respond to their fans. I learned some valuable lessons from those letters that I still hold dear to my heart to this very day:

1. Tom Araya had mad female fans in Ohio who wanted to have his child.
2. It was easy to pretend to be Tom Araya when calling fans who gave out their phone numbers and asked Tom to call them.
3. It was an automatic that fans would herald the praises of the double bass drumming of Dave Lombardo.
4. Slayer fans wanted all sorts of things from the band, down to used toothpicks, empty bottles from backstage (because we all know that the artists keep the empty bottles of booze they guzzle after a show, knowing that a fan is going to want them to UPS it), and one girl (who was also from Ohio) requested a vial of Tom's semen.
5. Slayer's fans are out of their fucking minds!

Thanks, Slayer fans, for some great times.

NOTICE

Employees Must Carve Slayer Into Forearm Before Returning to Work

BLABBERMOUTH.NET®

USER [_____]
PASS [_____]

LOG IN TO POST!

☐ Remember Me

RETRIEVE PASSWORD

SEARCH NEWS
[search text]

GO!

SEARCH CD REVIEWS
[search text]

GO!

LATEST NEWS

Last U

DEEP PURPLE Singer On Band's Lc Hall Of Fame' Nomination - Nov. 22,

GEOFF TATE On Split With QUEENSI Nov. 22, 2012

HAMMERFALL, THERION, Ex-EUROP Swedish Version Of 'Rock Of Ages' M

BUTCHER BABIES Interviewed By (Video) - Nov. 22, 2012

BACKSTREET ME

BEST METAL BLOGS

Call them blogs, websites, whatever, but these destinations are the modern-day versions of tape trading, fanzines, and college radio, combined into one wonderfully opinionated blob of information. Here are ten winners:

1. Blabbermouth.net (Blabbermouth)
2. Metalsludge.tv (Metal Sludge)
3. Metalsucks.net (MetalSucks)
4. TheMetalinquisition.com (Metal Inquisition)
5. Decibelmagazine.com/blog (Deciblog)
6. Zenametal.blogspot.com (Zena Metal Wants to Conquer the World)
7. Metalinjection.net (Metal Injection)
8. Heavymetaladdiction.com (Heavy Metal Addiction)
9. Noisecreep.com (Noisecreep)
10. Bravewords.com (Brave Words & Bloody Knuckles)

HEAVY METAL READING LIST

Contrary to popular belief, Metalheads DO in fact read books. How in the world do you think the Metal elders discovered all of the wizardry and dragons and Norse mythology in their lyrics? Wikipedia??? Nope. They read books, sometimes obsessively. So, now that there are a plethora of books covering the subject of Heavy Metal and its respective players, which are the best? Which is the worst? Well, we're gonna tell you. As in, right now!

1. **LORDS OF CHAOS: THE BLOODY RISE OF THE SATANIC METAL UNDERGROUND**
   Michael Moynihan's fascinating peek inside the notorious Norwegian Black Metal scene is chock-full of Satanism, arson, murder . . . and that's just pertaining to the band members from such legendary groups as Mayhem, Immortal, Emperor, Darkthrone, and, of course, Burzum. All bullshit aside, this is a must-read for any passionate fan of independent music and its surrounding community, let alone Black Metal enthusiasts.

2. **SOUND OF THE BEAST: THE COMPLETE HEADBANGING HISTORY OF HEAVY METAL**
   Ian Christe does an excellent job with this, not only chronicling Metal's vast history, but also enhancing it with interviews and other great bits of information. Very well put together.

3. **LEMMY: WHITE LINE FEVER**
   Ah, Lemmy . . . notorious, infamous, and legendary, as is the story of his life. *White Line Fever*'s got the whole warts-'n-all (literally) tale, and it is delivered in the voice of the man who lived it—and lived it he has. We swear, you can hear Lemmy's gravelly, Brit accent as you go from page to page. The ultimate in sex, drugs, and rock 'n' roll. Everyone else is a poser.

4. **THE HEROIN DIARIES: A YEAR IN THE LIFE OF A SHATTERED ROCK STAR**
   Nikki Sixx's debauchery, as well as that of his Mötley bandmates, is well documented; however, this shit is just beyond. If even 10 percent of this book is true, Nikki is clearly one of the most fucked-up individuals to ever walk the earth . . . and live.

5. **HEAVY METAL FUN TIME ACTIVITY BOOK**
   We feel like one of these should be left at every table in every coffee shop in Amsterdam. You can color, solve puzzles, do some Sudoku . . . Fun for the whole family . . . or just stoned Metalheads.

6. **MURDER IN THE FRONT ROW: SHOTS FROM THE BAY AREA THRASH METAL EPICENTER**
   For those of us who reside three thousand miles from the capital of Thrash Metal, Harald Oimoen and Brian Lew give us a little visual taste of the history of its scene. The bands, the fans, the sweat, and the blood. A must-have for any real Metal fan.

7. **TO LIVE IS TO DIE: THE LIFE AND DEATH OF METALLICA'S CLIFF BURTON**

Joel McIver simply nails it with this book in telling the Metallica portion of Cliff's story, but even more impressive is his in-depth view of Cliff the musician, as well as Cliff the man. Anything and everything you could possibly want to know about Cliff Burton lies within these pages. A fantastic read.

8. **REIGN IN BLOOD (33⅓)**

We love the 33⅓ series, and when we learned of this edition, you can only imagine how fast we ran to the bookstore. D. X. Ferris's start-to-finish detailing of the buildup to, the making of, and the aftermath of the most incredible Thrash album ever recorded. Great!

9. **IRON MAIDEN: A PHOTO HISTORY**

Ross Halfin's name is synonymous with Heavy Metal photography, and this 240-page gem features amazing shots of the one-and-only Iron Maiden throughout their career. Ross has been shooting them since forever, and he captures the majesty of the band like no other photog. Beautifully done.

10. **MUSTAINE: A HEAVY METAL MEMOIR**

This here is the only book on this list that is 100 percent unadulterated garbage! Anything you've ever heard or has been rumored about Dave Mustaine that makes you dislike him plays out in this "memoir." The biggest problem is that you won't believe a word Dave is saying from page one, and that will just give your distaste for the guy even more strength. Try telling the truth sometime, Dave.

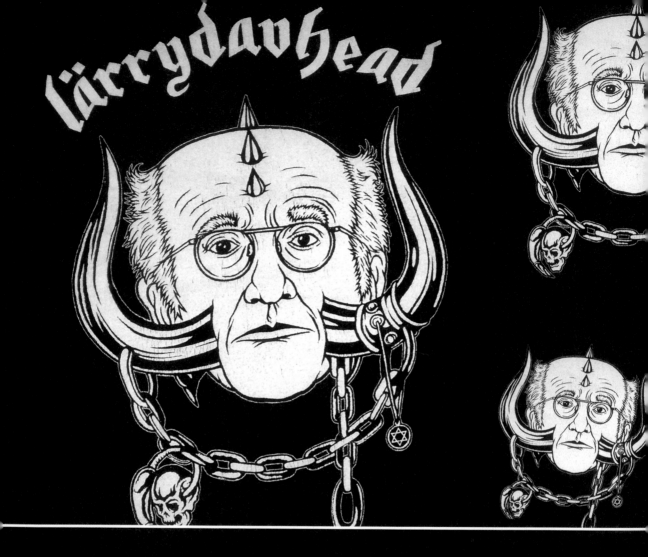

HEAVY METAL FUN TIME

10 ILLEGIBLE BLACK METAL LOGOS (RORSCHACH TESTS?)

Frankly, these disasterpieces deserve a book of their very own. We were always taught that if it looks good on a T-shirt, it's a great logo. These happen to look like total ass no matter where you put them. In fact, if a psychiatrist were to put any of these in front of you—say during some sort of evaluation to determine whether or not you're capable of standing trial for a string of church burnings, or perhaps a murder or two—they could easily be utilized as effective Rorschach tests. While we WILL play the role of spoiler and let you in on which bands' logos these are, we shall also throw you our Rorschach-like interpretations of these bad boys. Check it:

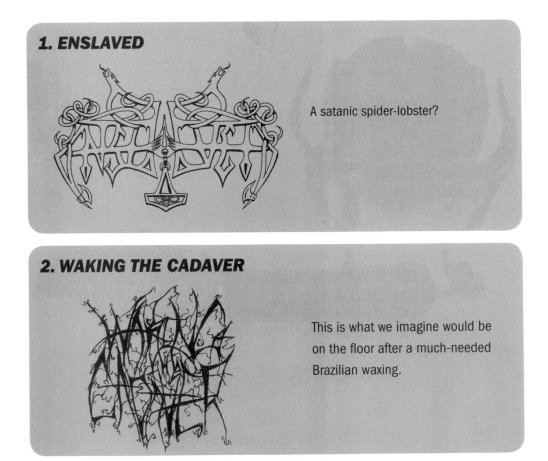

1. ENSLAVED

A satanic spider-lobster?

2. WAKING THE CADAVER

This is what we imagine would be on the floor after a much-needed Brazilian waxing.

3. BAZZAH

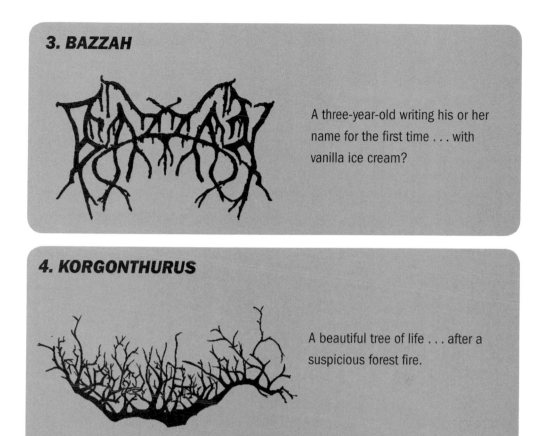

A three-year-old writing his or her name for the first time . . . with vanilla ice cream?

4. KORGONTHURUS

A beautiful tree of life . . . after a suspicious forest fire.

5. XASTHUR

A photo of a lovely gothic brooch taken at an extremely slow shutter speed.

6. FORGOTTEN LAND

A shitty-looking forest atop a shittier Black Metal logo.

7. NAGLFAR

Post–extreme weight gain tramp stamp of . . . something.

8. BLOODBATH

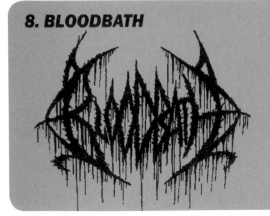

A piece of paper with black crayon covering white crayon that's been scratched randomly with a quarter.

9. LEVIATHAN

A semi-legible crescent moon over a primitive Jackson Pollock.

10. THE MERCILESS BOOK OF METAL LISTS

. . . if it were designed as a Black Metal logo

A MERCILESS METAL CROSSWORD PUZZLE

ACROSS

4 Mayhem guitarist
6 Homemade music magazine
7 An NWOBHM band, as well as a luxury car
9 Chicago Christian Doom Metal band
10 Mötley Crüe and Motörhead use this in their names
13 Missing a few finger tips, but he helped invent Heavy Metal
15 The Ripper who replaced Rob in Priest
16 King Diamond's birth first name
17 Carnivore/Type O frontman's early stage name
19 Some Kind of (Nightmare for Dave Mustaine) film
22 "Out"-there vocalist for Gorgoroth
23 Ozzy's elfin Sabbath replacement
24 Lips's band
26 Black Metal's true originators
28 Swedish Blackmore wannabe
30 First label to release a Metallica album
32 Former Anthrax guitarist or Olympic swimmer
33 The best NWOBHM Head
36 Grindcore's record label home
38 Ozzy's bitchy wife
39 Created Death Metal's goriest album art
40 Black Metallers (among others) HATE these people
41 Roadrunner Records' short-lived hardcore imprint
42 Swedish band that released "Chaosphere" in 1998

DOWN

1 Lemmy's pre-Motörhead psychedelic band
2 Tom Araya made a cameo in this Suicidal Tendencies video
3 Slayer's evil has none of these
5 Paul Di'Anno's post-Maiden band
8 Maiden's eventually released demo
11 Iced Earth plays this brand of Metal
12 Bathory's deceased founder
14 Long-running UK Monsters of Rock festival location
18 Strapping Young Guitarist
20 Max, Igor & co.'s second album
21 The best lesson Paul Baloff taught was in this
25 Manowar HATES this kind of Metal
27 Cliff Burton helped put this ghoulish punk band back on the map
29 Scott Ian's wacky adopted slogan
31 Didn't burn, but created "Seven Churches"
34 Saxon's classic "Denim & _____"
35 These Germans played as fast as sharks
37 Venom's preying original guitarist

THE MERCILESS AFTERWORD
BY PHILIP H. ANSELMO

Discovering music in one's life is a diverse and personal thing. And every music fan experiences in their own way how they actually got into the genre(s) as a passion, and it's hardly ever in a perfect time line as to the actual date the music came out. We hear music when we do, and take to it in time, or not. Music is older than all of us, so its history is ours to writhe in and absorb.

I am an unabashed Heavy Metal fan. And I know as well as anyone that Metal fans can be an extremely loyal lot. But we are a very critical lot too, as the genres of Metal and its cavalcade of subgenres constantly pop up and the need for more extremities are met. With each new movement, a new, defiant, outspoken, and sovereign audience is born.

Speaking from my own experiences back when I was a young Metal fan, I clearly remember how the acquired skill (and love) of needing music to be faster and heavier claimed me as a willing victim. And once this happened in my life, a falling domino effect of "List Making" begat a shitload of bands that'd eventually be lumped into some sort of genre and put on one of my many cassette compilation tapes.

There were two major instances in my life that "changed me" as a young Metal fan, or more accurately, helped mold me into the forty-four-year-old lover-of-odes-to-Lucifer that I am today.

The first was in 1982, at a time when I'd become best friends with a dude named Thomas Grimoskas. We had spotted each other in the small neighborhood we lived in, and made an instant connection because we were both wearing Iron Maiden T-shirts. We were, to my recollection, the only young cats in this micro-part of New Orleans to even own Maiden shirts.

Incidentally, Thomas was a drummer, and I knew in my heart I was a singer, but at that point I hadn't sung a damn note in a practice room with any "real" band. But based upon our mutual musical diggings, Thomas and I formed a band, my first "real" band. But this is hardly the point.

To get to the bulk of it all, during our time hanging out "in a band," listening to music and absorbing influences became mandatory. And discovering new bands, especially occult-driven bands for some reason or another, became a joint passion that escalated into an excitable sort of competition between him and me over "who could turn who" onto the "Heaviest" stuff.

We were both huge Black Sabbath fans, and Ozzy Osbourne had released his two inspired solo efforts with Randy Rhoads. But Osbourne's Aleister Crowley–lifted *Diary of a Madman* was our favorite of the two, so our adoration for all things pretentiously and potentially dark in music had already been deeply ingrained into our approach as to deciding what was acceptable, or not.

I remember Thomas calling my house after school one day (we went to different schools), and he simply said, "Man, you gotta get over here!" and I knew what that meant. He'd found a new band that I needed to check out. That band was Venom, and the album was *Black Metal*. It isn't important that we'd missed Venom's first record, *Welcome to Hell* . . . because we didn't know it existed yet.

You got what you got in New Orleans record stores back in the infantile stages of underground Metal in the early '80s. Chances are, *Welcome to Hell* wasn't even carried in many, if any, stores in the area, or we could've just missed it haphazardly with the burdens of school and after-school jobs eating up precious time and facilitating lost opportunities.

Needless to say, Venom's *Black Metal* was our initiation into this life-changing musical expression, and it still serves as a youthful reminder, even to this very day.

What struck me first and foremost was *Black Metal*'s cover art; it affected me a great deal. From the now-famous goat head printed in a metallic silver over its black background, which I now have proudly tattooed on my lower back, to the lyrical quote on the back of the album's cover about drinking "the vomit of the priests," etc., to the band photos. Never before had I come across a band pushing these types of over-the-top "Evil" visual extremities.

The image of Cronos writhing in the middle of a candle-adorned pentagram, and Mantas sitting on a cheesy motorcycle in front of a wall of amps with his hair blowing in the "wind," and a scowling Abaddon decked out in leather with chained Rottweilers in tow is still etched into my memory bank. There was also a poster and lyric sheet inside the original *Black Metal* album, which were always killer bonuses for young record collectors back in the day.

But by fucking all that's unholy, it was the music that did permanent damage to my uninitiated mind. Never before in my life had I heard such blatantly satanic lyrics delivered in such guttural bellows devoid of melody. The sound of the record, production-wise, was like being attached to the front grille of a bulldozer: hideous, overpowering, and head crushing. Never had a record made me feel actually, and accurately, nauseated! It was true!

At first I wasn't sure if I hated it or loved it, but the sheer impact of the record was impossible to ignore. There was a vulgarity within the grooves of the album that made me mentally flinch! I wasn't raised in a religious house, by any standard of the imagination, but somehow Venom's absolute disdain for all things Christian tweaked something deep in my heart.

Remember, I was at a young and impressionable age. Despite the obvious cornball shallowness of Venom's primitive message, at the time, I took their jabs at socially palpable religion very seriously. To me, it was as if the band had captured on vinyl the feeling of the film *The Exorcist*. For as young as I was, there wasn't a scarier religiously based flick out there. And I loved the fucking movie, and still do.

So, in turn, revolt and quasi-religious guilt soon wavered, and in its place bloomed a stark excitement unlike anything I'd experienced musically up to that point in my life. It was a gloriously rebellious feeling! It was liberating! It was an exclusive musical statement far removed from my parents' old rock record collection, or the Metal classics I'd come to love after them. I had found a boundaryless feeling spawned from that slab of Venom vinyl, and like my love for horror movies, there was no turning back now that this new genre's vein was tapped. I still had a great love for Motörhead, Judas Priest, and Iron Maiden, but the raw power of Venom was a completely different beast that spoke to a different part of my heart.

As things would pan out, like most other extreme or Metal music collectors out there, I needed more! The faster the better! The slower the heavier! The heavier and faster the better! The more satanic and/or anti-Christian the better!

Shortly after I'd discovered Venom, it seemed that new genres of bands (see Speed Metal, Thrash Metal, and satanic Metal/Venom clones) were popping up one after the fucking other. Metal production was going through a major change as well, oftentimes for the worse, depending on one's view.

But then I heard Slayer, and everything changed. This was the second great epiphany for me in Metal music. Truth be told, at first, I didn't quite know what to think of Slayer . . .

As I've mentioned, Metal production was changing rapidly. And it was Metallica's *Kill 'Em All* record from 1983 that upped the crunch in axe tones significantly and began the wave of actual '80s Thrash Metal to my ears. James Hetfield's right-hand chops were also a mighty thing to behold. Fellow Bay Area thrashers Exodus had a crunchy tone on their awesome *Bonded by Blood* LP, recorded in '84, but it suffered from an otherwise cluttered drum sound. Anthrax's *Fistful of Metal* was a great example of speedy, crunchy Thrash in '84, with excellent drumsmanship, yet it flaunted high-pitched falsetto vocals, which could have been a turnoff for some listeners at this point in time. And excellent drum tones really seemed to be commonplace with bands from Canada, like Exciter's '84 effort, *Violence & Force*, and even earlier, Anvil's '83 slab, *Forged in Fire*.

There was a need, as a listener, to eventually unite these separate sounds and styles. And, at the time, the faster the band played, the better. But speed for the sake of speed in the ranks of Metal in the early to mid-'80s would eventually fall squarely on the shoulders of Slayer.

However, despite their intensity, as I've mentioned, I hadn't figured Slayer out yet. All I'd heard was the song "Aggressive Perfector" off of Metal Blade's 1983 *Metal Massacre III* compilation record, and their first full-length release, also from '83, *Show No Mercy.*

Unquestionably, Slayer had excellent songs, but the production, guitar sounds, and drum sounds were subpar to my youthful "example-based" ears. A glimmer of hope came in the dose of their now-famous EP *Haunting the Chapel* (1984), where the axe tones were better and the songs more hellacious, but still, the guitar sounds were not quite up to par with the crunchy tones Metallica were putting out.

And this bothered me at the time, because although Metallica, Exodus, and Anthrax had made their respective marks, none of them were occult-themed to an extreme the way Venom were. I needed a new void filled. Slayer were definitely pushing the satanic shtick full throttle, and in my heart, I wished they would take a cue from Metallica's guitar sounds. As history shows, most bands sure fucking did. And in time, occult themed or not, bands by the droves followed suit.

Just like my first experience with the aforementioned Venom, my bud Thomas came to the rescue for my second never-dead moment in time with one of his "Get over here now!" phone calls.

This was when I heard Slayer's 1985 offering, *Hell Awaits*, for the first time, and from that point on, there was no second-guessing the sheer, unforgiving brutality of this band. The guitar sounds had the crunch that was badly needed. The lead guitar solos reminded me of a cross between the dueling solos of Judas Priest meets what Greg Ginn brought to the table with Black Flag, except with more hyper-speed lunacy. The drums were fast as fuck, reverb soaked, and relentless. And the lyrical message belted out by vocalist Tom Araya was more blasphemous, over-pronounced, and hateful than ever.

If Venom's *Black Metal* was *The Exorcist* of music for me, then Slayer's *Hell Awaits* was the musical equivalent to the ultra-gory and inspirational flick *The Evil Dead*, with the band's chanting of "Join us . . . " recorded backward and forward.

There are times in life when things fall into place PERFECTLY. There was no more perfect mixture of music-driven emotion, teen rebelliousness, and socially outcasting adulation for what a band was doing at the time. Repeated listens produced the ability to consume it and truly understand the meaning of "Heavy." Experiencing Slayer's *Hell Awaits* was the perfect storm. Period.

As history rolls, the answer to Venom and Slayer came by the hundreds over a short period of time. Bands, in no particular order, like Hellhammer, Celtic Frost, Kreator, Sepultura, Infernal Majesty, Bathory, Sodom, Possessed, Sadus, Sarcófago, Dark Angel, Destruction, and so on took the formulas and ran. Waiting in the wings would be late '80s Death Metal, then Grindcore, then early '90s Black Metal, and then the ever-quivering mass of subgenres that are percolating around the globe today. And you gotta love it.

Long live list makers, odes to Catholic hell and nationalistic hymns of blackened defiance, unorthodox Black Noise thinkers, and the bands before "the bands" before "the bands," whenever the hell they came out, that have the likes of us in check. Tirade over.

—Philip H. Anselmo

ACKNOWLEDGMENTS

HOWIE & SACHA WOULD SINCERELY LIKE TO THANK:

KAVES, for being a great friend and a great connector; Robert Guinsler—the MAN who made the magic happen; our editor, David Cashion, who understood our mission and supported us from ground, air, and sea & everyone at Abrams Books; Donna McLeer/Tunnel Vizion for being our stylist; Maria Ferrero/Adrenaline PR for simply being the BEST; Philip Anselmo, Kerry King, Frank White, Ed Esposito, Stephanie Cabral, Danny Lilker, Monte Conner, Borivoj Krgin, Shaun Glass, Max and Gloria Cavalera, Jon and Marsha Zazula, Eddie Trunk, Richard Christy, Hoya Roc, Katon W. De Pena, Brian Slagel, Scott Ian, Flemming Rasmussen, Mass Ebdrup, Kristen Mulderig, Gary Holt, Betsy Weiss, MC Serch, John Gallagher, Kate Richardson, and all the Metalheads for being true to yourselves since day one. Metal up everyone's ass!

HOWIE

Big Up: Sacha Jenkins for making things happen as only you can; ILL BILL—thanks for the inspiration, contributions, and the friendship; and you—for taking the time to read this!

I dedicate this book, and everything I do, for that matter, to my beautiful wife, Julie, and my gorgeous little girl, Nia. Together, you are everything to me.

Dear Mom and Dad,

Remember all those times I stayed out until the sun was already up? Those mornings when I was heading to bed as you were just waking up and all of the ice cream had been eaten? I'm not sure I ever got to say thank you for you putting up with all of that, so I will do so here and now. THANK YOU!!! I love you both and miss you dearly.

SACHA

Thanks to: Raquel, Djali, my main man Marceau Aguila Jenkins-Cepeda, ego trip, Mass Appeal, Decon, the White Mandingos, Tony, Bill, Geezer and Ozzy—for always keeping my Sabbaths unquestionably BLACK—and last but not least, Howie Abrams: a man who hasn't lost his connection to what inspires him, while keepin' it geek chic all the way.

ABOUT THE AUTHORS

HOWIE ABRAMS

Howie is a former...lots of things, including record label A&R rep, music publisher, artist manager and children's party performer (he wore a Mickey Mouse costume at his niece's first birthday party) among others. Apparently, he's just co-written a book. Abrams grew up in his beloved NYC as part of it's Metal and Hardcore scenes and has always carried the torch for aggressive music. Today he manages a tattoo shop in Brooklyn and loves his wife and daughter on an unfathomable level.

SACHA JENKINS

Sacha Jenkins loves heavy music. He grew up in New York City. He has produced some books--some about hip hop, some about graffiti. He's produced some television too. He plays guitar in a band. The bass player from Bad Brains is in that band. Jenkins is also a husband and father.